TEACHER'S PET PUBLICATIONS

PUZZLE PACK
for
Great Expectations

based on the book by
Charles Dickens

Written by
William T. Collins

© 2005 Teacher's Pet Publications
All Rights Reserved

The materials in this packet are copyrighted
by Teacher's Pet Publications, Inc.

These pages may be duplicated by the purchaser
for use in the purchaser's own classroom.

Copying any of these materials and distributing them
for any other purpose is a violation of the copyright laws.

© 2005 Teacher's Pet Publications, Inc.
www.tpet.com

INTRODUCTION
If you already own the LitPlan for this title, this Puzzle Pack will refresh your Unit Resource Materials and Vocabulary Resource Materials sections plus give you additional materials you can substitute into the tests. If you do not already have a complete LitPlan, these pages will give you some supplemental materials to use with your own plan. There are two main groups of materials: one set for unit words (such as characters' names, symbols, places, etc.) and one set for vocabulary words associated with the book.

WORD LIST
There is a word list for both the unit words and the vocabulary words. These lists show you which words are being used in the materials and the clues or definitions being used for those words. You may want to give students a word list with clues/definitions to help them, or you may want students to only have a word list (without clues/definitions) if you want them to work a little harder. Both are available for duplication. The word lists can also be your "calling key" for the bingo games.

FILL IN THE BLANK AND MATCHING
There are 4 each of the fill in the blank and matching worksheets for both the unit and vocabulary words. These pages can be used either as extra worksheets for students or as objective parts of a unit test. They can be done individually if students need extra help or as a whole class activity to review the material covered.

MAGIC SQUARES
The magic squares not only reinforce the material covered but also work on reasoning and math skills. Many teachers have told us that their students really enjoy doing these!

WORD SEARCH PUZZLES
The word search words go in all directions, as indicated on your answer keys. Two of the word search puzzles have the clues listed rather than the words. This makes the puzzle a little more difficult, but it reinforces the material better. Two word search puzzles have words only for students who find the clue puzzles too difficult.

CROSSWORD PUZZLES
Both unit and vocabulary word sections have 4 crossword puzzles.

BINGO CARDS
There are 32 individual bingo cards for the unit words and 32 individual bingo cards for the vocabulary words. You can use your word list as a "call list," calling the words at random and marking them off of your list as you go, or you could use the flash cards by cutting them apart and drawing the words at random from a hat (or box or whatever). To make a better review, you might ask for the definition and spelling of each word as you call it out–or you could call out the definitions and have students tell you the words they need to look for on the puzzle.

JUGGLE LETTERS
The vocabulary juggle letter game is intended to help students learn the spellings of the words. One sheet has the definitions listed on it as an extra help for students who need it or to reinforce the definitions if you choose to do so.

FLASH CARDS
We've included a set of vocabulary flash cards you can duplicate, cut, and fold for your students. Some teachers make a few sets for general use by the class; others make a set for each student. Some teachers duplicate them for each student and have the students cut & fold their own. You can cut out just the words and put them in a hat, have each student pick out one word and write the definition and a sentence for that word. Students then swap words and papers, with the next student adding a sentence of his own under the last one. You can have students swap as many times as you like. Each time the student will read the sentences written prior to his own and then add a sentence. You can cut out the words and definitions separately and play "I Have; Who Has?" Each student in the room draws a word and definition. The first student says, "I have (the name of the word). Who has the definition?" The student with the definition reads it then says, "I have (the name of the vocabulary word she has). Who has the definition?" The round continues until all words and definitions have been given.

Great Expectations Unit Word List

No.	Word	Clue/Definition
1.	AGED P	Wemmick's father
2.	AVENGER	Pip's servant
3.	BARGEMEN	Three Jolly _____
4.	BIDDY	Pip's confidant at the Gargery's
5.	BIRTHDAY	Camilla, Raymond & Sara visit Miss H on this day every year
6.	BLACKSMITH	Joe's occupation
7.	BRAG	'_____ is a good dog, but Holdfast is a better.'
8.	CLARA	Herbert's girlfriend, later his wife
9.	CLOTHES	'I'm all wrong in these ____.' (Joe said to Pip)
10.	COMPEYSON	Enemy of Magwitch; jilted Miss H
11.	DICKENS	Author
12.	DRUMMLE	Marries Estella
13.	ESTELLA	Miss Havisham's adopted daughter
14.	EXPECTATIONS	Great _____
15.	FIRE	It burned Miss H and Pip
16.	GARGERY	Joe's last name
17.	GRAVEYARD	Pip meets a convict there
18.	GRAVY	Joe gives Pip extra ___ at dinner with Mr. P
19.	GREAT	____ Expectations
20.	HAND	Pip and Joe were 'Brought up by ____'
21.	HAVISHAM	Spinster woman who uses Pip
22.	HERBERT	The 'pale young gentleman'; Pip's flatmate
23.	JAGGERS	Pip's guardian
24.	JOE	Pip's blacksmith brother-in-law
25.	JOLLY	Three _____ Bargemen
26.	LONDON	Jaggers's office is in this city
27.	MAGWITCH	Pip's benefactor
28.	MOLLY	Estella's mother; Jagger's servant
29.	MRS JOE	Pip's sister
30.	ORLICK	Tries to kill Pip
31.	PIE	Pip took pork ___ to give to the convict
32.	PIP	He has great expectations
33.	PORTER	Orlick's position at Miss H's house
34.	POSITION	Pip bought one for Herbert so he would have a steady income
35.	PROVIS	Magwitch's assumed name
36.	PUMBLECHOOK	Claimed to be the founder of Pip's fortunes
37.	STARTOP	Helped Pip and Herbert; former roommate
38.	TRABB	The letter from ___ & Co. brought news of Mrs. Joe's death
39.	TUTOR	Matthew Pocket to Pip; educator
40.	WEMMICK	Jaggers's clerk
41.	WOPSLE	Church clerk turned actor

Copyrighted

Great Expectations Fill In The Blank 1

_____ 1. Marries Estella

_____ 2. Pip's benefactor

_____ 3. The 'pale young gentleman'; Pip's flatmate

_____ 4. Three _____ Bargemen

_____ 5. Pip's guardian

_____ 6. Claimed to be the founder of Pip's fortunes

_____ 7. Pip took pork ___ to give to the convict

_____ 8. Orlick's position at Miss H's house

_____ 9. Spinster woman who uses Pip

_____ 10. Herbert's girlfriend, later his wife

_____ 11. He has great expectations

_____ 12. It burned Miss H and Pip

_____ 13. Pip's confidant at the Gargery's

_____ 14. Estella's mother; Jagger's servant

_____ 15. Camilla, Raymond & Sara visit Miss H on this day every year

_____ 16. Magwitch's assumed name

_____ 17. Church clerk turned actor

_____ 18. Wemmick's father

_____ 19. Pip's blacksmith brother-in-law

_____ 20. Author

Great Expectations Fill In The Blank 1 Answer Key

DRUMMLE	1. Marries Estella
MAGWITCH	2. Pip's benefactor
HERBERT	3. The 'pale young gentleman'; Pip's flatmate
JOLLY	4. Three _____ Bargemen
JAGGERS	5. Pip's guardian
PUMBLECHOOK	6. Claimed to be the founder of Pip's fortunes
PIE	7. Pip took pork ___ to give to the convict
PORTER	8. Orlick's position at Miss H's house
HAVISHAM	9. Spinster woman who uses Pip
CLARA	10. Herbert's girlfriend, later his wife
PIP	11. He has great expectations
FIRE	12. It burned Miss H and Pip
BIDDY	13. Pip's confidant at the Gargery's
MOLLY	14. Estella's mother; Jagger's servant
BIRTHDAY	15. Camilla, Raymond & Sara visit Miss H on this day every year
PROVIS	16. Magwitch's assumed name
WOPSLE	17. Church clerk turned actor
AGED P	18. Wemmick's father
JOE	19. Pip's blacksmith brother-in-law
DICKENS	20. Author

Great Expectations Fill In The Blank 2

1. Pip's servant
2. The letter from ___ & Co. brought news of Mrs. Joe's death
3. Enemy of Magwitch; jilted Miss H
4. Joe gives Pip extra ___ at dinner with Mr. P
5. Church clerk turned actor
6. Tries to kill Pip
7. Jaggers's office is in this city
8. Orlick's position at Miss H's house
9. Herbert's girlfriend, later his wife
10. Jaggers's clerk
11. Helped Pip and Herbert; former roommate
12. He has great expectations
13. Claimed to be the founder of Pip's fortunes
14. Author
15. Three Jolly _____
16. Marries Estella
17. Pip and Joe were 'Brought up by ____'
18. Pip's blacksmith brother-in-law
19. Pip's confidant at the Gargery's
20. Wemmick's father

Great Expectations Fil In The Blank 4 Answer Key

AVENGER	1. Pip's servant
TRABB	2. The letter from ___ & Co. brought news of Mrs. Joe's death
COMPEYSON	3. Enemy of Magwitch; jilted Miss H
GRAVY	4. Joe gives Pip extra ___ at dinner with Mr. P
WOPSLE	5. Church clerk turned actor
ORLICK	6. Tries to kill Pip
LONDON	7. Jaggers's office is in this city
PORTER	8. Orlick's position at Miss H's house
CLARA	9. Herbert's girlfriend, later his wife
WEMMICK	10. Jaggers's clerk
STARTOP	11. Helped Pip and Herbert; former roommate
PIP	12. He has great expectations
PUMBLECHOOK	13. Claimed to be the founder of Pip's fortunes
DICKENS	14. Author
BARGEMEN	15. Three Jolly _____
DRUMMLE	16. Marries Estella
HAND	17. Pip and Joe were 'Brought up by ____'
JOE	18. Pip's blacksmith brother-in-law
BIDDY	19. Pip's confidant at the Gargery's
AGED P	20. Wemmick's father

Great Expectations Fill In The Blank 3

1. ____ Expectations
2. Estella's mother; Jagger's servant
3. Joe's last name
4. Jaggers's clerk
5. Church clerk turned actor
6. Spinster woman who uses Pip
7. The 'pale young gentleman'; Pip's flatmate
8. Orlick's position at Miss H's house
9. Claimed to be the founder of Pip's fortunes
10. Pip bought one for Herbert so he would have a steady income
11. Miss Havisham's adopted daughter
12. Camilla, Raymond & Sara visit Miss H on this day every year
13. Jaggers's office is in this city
14. Three _____ Bargemen
15. Author
16. Matthew Pocket to Pip; educator
17. Joe gives Pip extra ___ at dinner with Mr. P
18. Pip took pork ___ to give to the convict
19. '_____ is a good dog, but Holdfast is a better.'
20. Pip's sister

Great Expectations Fill In The Blank 3 Answer Key

GREAT	1. ____ Expectations
MOLLY	2. Estella's mother; Jagger's servant
GARGERY	3. Joe's last name
WEMMICK	4. Jaggers's clerk
WOPSLE	5. Church clerk turned actor
HAVISHAM	6. Spinster woman who uses Pip
HERBERT	7. The 'pale young gentleman'; Pip's flatmate
PORTER	8. Orlick's position at Miss H's house
PUMBLECHOOK	9. Claimed to be the founder of Pip's fortunes
POSITION	10. Pip bought one for Herbert so he would have a steady income
ESTELLA	11. Miss Havisham's adopted daughter
BIRTHDAY	12. Camilla, Raymond & Sara visit Miss H on this day every year
LONDON	13. Jaggers's office is in this city
JOLLY	14. Three ____ Bargemen
DICKENS	15. Author
TUTOR	16. Matthew Pocket to Pip; educator
GRAVY	17. Joe gives Pip extra ___ at dinner with Mr. P
PIE	18. Pip took pork ___ to give to the convict
BRAG	19. '____ is a good dog, but Holdfast is a better.'
MRS JOE	20. Pip's sister

Great Expectations Fill In The Blank 4

1. Helped Pip and Herbert; former roommate
2. Marries Estella
3. Estella's mother; Jagger's servant
4. Orlick's position at Miss H's house
5. Great _____
6. Author
7. Joe's last name
8. Pip bought one for Herbert so he would have a steady income
9. Joe gives Pip extra ___ at dinner with Mr. P
10. Camilla, Raymond & Sara visit Miss H on this day every year
11. 'I'm all wrong in these ____.' (Joe said to Pip)
12. Wemmick's father
13. Spinster woman who uses Pip
14. Tries to kill Pip
15. Pip's servant
16. Miss Havisham's adopted daughter
17. Magwitch's assumed name
18. Three Jolly _____
19. Claimed to be the founder of Pip's fortunes
20. Church clerk turned actor

Great Expectations Fill In The Blank 4 Answer Key

STARTOP	1. Helped Pip and Herbert; former roommate
DRUMMLE	2. Marries Estella
MOLLY	3. Estella's mother; Jagger's servant
PORTER	4. Orlick's position at Miss H's house
EXPECTATIONS	5. Great _____
DICKENS	6. Author
GARGERY	7. Joe's last name
POSITION	8. Pip bought one for Herbert so he would have a steady income
GRAVY	9. Joe gives Pip extra ___ at dinner with Mr. P
BIRTHDAY	10. Camilla, Raymond & Sara visit Miss H on this day every year
CLOTHES	11. 'I'm all wrong in these ____.' (Joe said to Pip)
AGED P	12. Wemmick's father
HAVISHAM	13. Spinster woman who uses Pip
ORLICK	14. Tries to kill Pip
AVENGER	15. Pip's servant
ESTELLA	16. Miss Havisham's adopted daughter
PROVIS	17. Magwitch's assumed name
BARGEMEN	18. Three Jolly _____
PUMBLECHOOK	19. Claimed to be the founder of Pip's fortunes
WOPSLE	20. Church clerk turned actor

Great Expectations Matching 1

___ 1. PIP   A. ____ Expectations
___ 2. WEMMICK   B. Jaggers's clerk
___ 3. HAVISHAM   C. Tries to kill Pip
___ 4. TRABB   D. Three _____ Bargemen
___ 5. LONDON   E. Author
___ 6. JOE   F. Pip's blacksmith brother-in-law
___ 7. HAND   G. Matthew Pocket to Pip; educator
___ 8. JAGGERS   H. Pip's benefactor
___ 9. EXPECTATIONS I. The letter from ___ & Co. brought news of Mrs. Joe's death
___10. JOLLY   J. '_____ is a good dog, but Holdfast is a better.'
___11. BARGEMEN   K. Pip and Joe were 'Brought up by ____'
___12. DICKENS   L. Three Jolly _____
___13. HERBERT   M. Jaggers's office is in this city
___14. MAGWITCH   N. Estella's mother; Jagger's servant
___15. PORTER   O. Pip's sister
___16. BRAG   P. Pip bought one for Herbert so he would have a steady income
___17. GREAT   Q. Orlick's position at Miss H's house
___18. ORLICK   R. It burned Miss H and Pip
___19. FIRE   S. Great _____
___20. TUTOR   T. Helped Pip and Herbert; former roommate
___21. MOLLY   U. The 'pale young gentleman'; Pip's flatmate
___22. MRS JOE   V. Pip's guardian
___23. CLARA   W. Spinster woman who uses Pip
___24. POSITION   X. He has great expectations
___25. STARTOP   Y. Herbert's girlfriend, later his wife

Great Expectations Matching 1 Answer Key

X - 1.	PIP	A. ____ Expectations
B - 2.	WEMMICK	B. Jaggers's clerk
W - 3.	HAVISHAM	C. Tries to kill Pip
I - 4.	TRABB	D. Three _____ Bargemen
M - 5.	LONDON	E. Author
F - 6.	JOE	F. Pip's blacksmith brother-in-law
K - 7.	HAND	G. Matthew Pocket to Pip; educator
V - 8.	JAGGERS	H. Pip's benefactor
S - 9.	EXPECTATIONS	I. The letter from ___ & Co. brought news of Mrs. Joe's death
D - 10.	JOLLY	J. '_____ is a good dog, but Holdfast is a better.'
L - 11.	BARGEMEN	K. Pip and Joe were 'Brought up by ____'
E - 12.	DICKENS	L. Three Jolly _____
U - 13.	HERBERT	M. Jaggers's office is in this city
H - 14.	MAGWITCH	N. Estella's mother; Jagger's servant
Q - 15.	PORTER	O. Pip's sister
J - 16.	BRAG	P. Pip bought one for Herbert so he would have a steady income
A - 17.	GREAT	Q. Orlick's position at Miss H's house
C - 18.	ORLICK	R. It burned Miss H and Pip
R - 19.	FIRE	S. Great _____
G - 20.	TUTOR	T. Helped Pip and Herbert; former roommate
N - 21.	MOLLY	U. The 'pale young gentleman'; Pip's flatmate
O - 22.	MRS JOE	V. Pip's guardian
Y - 23.	CLARA	W. Spinster woman who uses Pip
P - 24.	POSITION	X. He has great expectations
T - 25.	STARTOP	Y. Herbert's girlfriend, later his wife

Great Expectations Matching 2

___ 1. PUMBLECHOOK   A. Magwitch's assumed name
___ 2. HERBERT   B. Miss Havisham's adopted daughter
___ 3. BARGEMEN   C. Claimed to be the founder of Pip's fortunes
___ 4. PROVIS   D. Enemy of Magwitch; jilted Miss H
___ 5. JOLLY   E. Estella's mother; Jagger's servant
___ 6. ESTELLA   F. Pip took pork ___ to give to the convict
___ 7. PIP   G. The letter from ___ & Co. brought news of Mrs. Joe's death
___ 8. POSITION   H. He has great expectations
___ 9. PORTER   I. Marries Estella
___ 10. PIE   J. Pip's sister
___ 11. AVENGER   K. Pip's servant
___ 12. DICKENS   L. Pip's benefactor
___ 13. DRUMMLE   M. Pip's guardian
___ 14. STARTOP   N. Pip bought one for Herbert so he would have a steady income
___ 15. MOLLY   O. Three _____ Bargemen
___ 16. CLARA   P. It burned Miss H and Pip
___ 17. FIRE   Q. Helped Pip and Herbert; former roommate
___ 18. COMPEYSON   R. Orlick's position at Miss H's house
___ 19. MRS JOE   S. Wemmick's father
___ 20. TRABB   T. Joe gives Pip extra ___ at dinner with Mr. P
___ 21. LONDON   U. Herbert's girlfriend, later his wife
___ 22. MAGWITCH   V. Jaggers's office is in this city
___ 23. JAGGERS   W. Three Jolly _____
___ 24. GRAVY   X. The 'pale young gentleman'; Pip's flatmate
___ 25. AGED P   Y. Author

Great Expectations Matching 2 Answer Key

C - 1. PUMBLECHOOK   A. Magwitch's assumed name
X - 2. HERBERT   B. Miss Havisham's adopted daughter
W - 3. BARGEMEN   C. Claimed to be the founder of Pip's fortunes
A - 4. PROVIS   D. Enemy of Magwitch; jilted Miss H
O - 5. JOLLY   E. Estella's mother; Jagger's servant
B - 6. ESTELLA   F. Pip took pork ___ to give to the convict
H - 7. PIP   G. The letter from ___ & Co. brought news of Mrs. Joe's death
N - 8. POSITION   H. He has great expectations
R - 9. PORTER   I. Marries Estella
F - 10. PIE   J. Pip's sister
K - 11. AVENGER   K. Pip's servant
Y - 12. DICKENS   L. Pip's benefactor
I - 13. DRUMMLE   M. Pip's guardian
Q - 14. STARTOP   N. Pip bought one for Herbert so he would have a steady income
E - 15. MOLLY   O. Three _____ Bargemen
U - 16. CLARA   P. It burned Miss H and Pip
P - 17. FIRE   Q. Helped Pip and Herbert; former roommate
D - 18. COMPEYSON   R. Orlick's position at Miss H's house
J - 19. MRS JOE   S. Wemmick's father
G - 20. TRABB   T. Joe gives Pip extra ___ at dinner with Mr. P
V - 21. LONDON   U. Herbert's girlfriend, later his wife
L - 22. MAGWITCH   V. Jaggers's office is in this city
M - 23. JAGGERS   W. Three Jolly _____
T - 24. GRAVY   X. The 'pale young gentleman'; Pip's flatmate
S - 25. AGED P   Y. Author

Great Expectations Matching 3

___ 1. MOLLY   A. Claimed to be the founder of Pip's fortunes
___ 2. AGED P   B. Wemmick's father
___ 3. MRS JOE   C. Magwitch's assumed name
___ 4. GRAVEYARD   D. Pip meets a convict there
___ 5. JAGGERS   E. Camilla, Raymond & Sara visit Miss H on this day every year
___ 6. AVENGER   F. Pip bought one for Herbert so he would have a steady income
___ 7. GARGERY   G. Enemy of Magwitch; jilted Miss H
___ 8. POSITION   H. Joe's last name
___ 9. ESTELLA   I. It burned Miss H and Pip
___10. TUTOR   J. Estella's mother; Jagger's servant
___11. FIRE   K. Pip's servant
___12. PIE   L. Author
___13. DICKENS   M. Miss Havisham's adopted daughter
___14. PROVIS   N. Jaggers's office is in this city
___15. CLARA   O. Matthew Pocket to Pip; educator
___16. CLOTHES   P. Three _____ Bargemen
___17. DRUMMLE   Q. The 'pale young gentleman'; Pip's flatmate
___18. MAGWITCH   R. Pip and Joe were 'Brought up by ____'
___19. JOLLY   S. 'I'm all wrong in these ____.' (Joe said to Pip)
___20. HAND   T. Marries Estella
___21. HERBERT   U. Pip's sister
___22. PUMBLECHOOK   V. Pip's benefactor
___23. COMPEYSON   W. Pip took pork ___ to give to the convict
___24. BIRTHDAY   X. Herbert's girlfriend, later his wife
___25. LONDON   Y. Pip's guardian

Great Expectations Matching 3 Answer Key

J - 1. MOLLY	A. Claimed to be the founder of Pip's fortunes
B - 2. AGED P	B. Wemmick's father
U - 3. MRS JOE	C. Magwitch's assumed name
D - 4. GRAVEYARD	D. Pip meets a convict there
Y - 5. JAGGERS	E. Camilla, Raymond & Sara visit Miss H on this day every year
K - 6. AVENGER	F. Pip bought one for Herbert so he would have a steady income
H - 7. GARGERY	G. Enemy of Magwitch; jilted Miss H
F - 8. POSITION	H. Joe's last name
M - 9. ESTELLA	I. It burned Miss H and Pip
O -10. TUTOR	J. Estella's mother; Jagger's servant
I - 11. FIRE	K. Pip's servant
W -12. PIE	L. Author
L - 13. DICKENS	M. Miss Havisham's adopted daughter
C -14. PROVIS	N. Jaggers's office is in this city
X -15. CLARA	O. Matthew Pocket to Pip; educator
S -16. CLOTHES	P. Three _____ Bargemen
T -17. DRUMMLE	Q. The 'pale young gentleman'; Pip's flatmate
V -18. MAGWITCH	R. Pip and Joe were 'Brought up by ____'
P -19. JOLLY	S. 'I'm all wrong in these ____.' (Joe said to Pip)
R -20. HAND	T. Marries Estella
Q -21. HERBERT	U. Pip's sister
A -22. PUMBLECHOOK	V. Pip's benefactor
G -23. COMPEYSON	W. Pip took pork ___ to give to the convict
E -24. BIRTHDAY	X. Herbert's girlfriend, later his wife
N -25. LONDON	Y. Pip's guardian

Great Expectations Matching 4

___ 1. MAGWITCH   A. The 'pale young gentleman'; Pip's flatmate
___ 2. ORLICK   B. Marries Estella
___ 3. LONDON   C. Pip's servant
___ 4. FIRE   D. Pip's benefactor
___ 5. TUTOR   E. Three Jolly _____
___ 6. COMPEYSON   F. It burned Miss H and Pip
___ 7. DRUMMLE   G. Magwitch's assumed name
___ 8. AGED P   H. Herbert's girlfriend, later his wife
___ 9. WEMMICK   I. Helped Pip and Herbert; former roommate
___10. WOPSLE   J. Orlick's position at Miss H's house
___11. AVENGER   K. Tries to kill Pip
___12. JAGGERS   L. Church clerk turned actor
___13. HERBERT   M. Pip's guardian
___14. HAVISHAM   N. Pip and Joe were 'Brought up by ____'
___15. JOLLY   O. Enemy of Magwitch; jilted Miss H
___16. ESTELLA   P. Matthew Pocket to Pip; educator
___17. CLARA   Q. Pip's sister
___18. STARTOP   R. Jaggers's clerk
___19. TRABB   S. Miss Havisham's adopted daughter
___20. BARGEMEN   T. Great _____
___21. MRS JOE   U. The letter from ___ & Co. brought news of Mrs. Joe's death
___22. PORTER   V. Jaggers's office is in this city
___23. PROVIS   W. Three _____ Bargemen
___24. HAND   X. Spinster woman who uses Pip
___25. EXPECTATIONS   Y. Wemmick's father

Great Expectations Matching 4 Answer Key

D - 1. MAGWITCH	A.	The 'pale young gentleman'; Pip's flatmate
K - 2. ORLICK	B.	Marries Estella
V - 3. LONDON	C.	Pip's servant
F - 4. FIRE	D.	Pip's benefactor
P - 5. TUTOR	E.	Three Jolly _____
O - 6. COMPEYSON	F.	It burned Miss H and Pip
B - 7. DRUMMLE	G.	Magwitch's assumed name
Y - 8. AGED P	H.	Herbert's girlfriend, later his wife
R - 9. WEMMICK	I.	Helped Pip and Herbert; former roommate
L - 10. WOPSLE	J.	Orlick's position at Miss H's house
C - 11. AVENGER	K.	Tries to kill Pip
M - 12. JAGGERS	L.	Church clerk turned actor
A - 13. HERBERT	M.	Pip's guardian
X - 14. HAVISHAM	N.	Pip and Joe were 'Brought up by ____'
W - 15. JOLLY	O.	Enemy of Magwitch; jilted Miss H
S - 16. ESTELLA	P.	Matthew Pocket to Pip; educator
H - 17. CLARA	Q.	Pip's sister
I - 18. STARTOP	R.	Jaggers's clerk
U - 19. TRABB	S.	Miss Havisham's adopted daughter
E - 20. BARGEMEN	T.	Great _____
Q - 21. MRS JOE	U.	The letter from ___ & Co. brought news of Mrs. Joe's death
J - 22. PORTER	V.	Jaggers's office is in this city
G - 23. PROVIS	W.	Three _____ Bargemen
N - 24. HAND	X.	Spinster woman who uses Pip
T - 25. EXPECTATIONS	Y.	Wemmick's father

Great Expectations Magic Squares 1

Match the definition with the vocabulary word. Put your answers in the magic squares below. When your answers are correct, all columns and rows will add to the same number.

A. TUTOR
B. MAGWITCH
C. ESTELLA
D. BARGEMEN
E. BLACKSMITH
F. MOLLY
G. STARTOP
H. HERBERT
I. GRAVEYARD
J. WOPSLE
K. HAND
L. FIRE
M. EXPECTATIONS
N. CLARA
O. BRAG
P. MRS JOE

1. Herbert's girlfriend, later his wife
2. Helped Pip and Herbert; former roommate
3. It burned Miss H and Pip
4. Matthew Pocket to Pip; educator
5. Pip and Joe were 'Brought up by ____'
6. Pip's benefactor
7. Great _____
8. The 'pale young gentleman'; Pip's flatmate
9. Joe's occupation
10. Pip's sister
11. Miss Havisham's adopted daughter
12. Church clerk turned actor
13. Three Jolly _____
14. Pip meets a convict there
15. Estella's mother; Jagger's servant
16. '_____ is a good dog, but Holdfast is a better.'

A=	B=	C=	D=
E=	F=	G=	H=
I=	J=	K=	L=
M=	N=	O=	P=

Great Expectations Magic Squares 1 Answer Key

Match the definition with the vocabulary word. Put your answers in the magic squares below. When your answers are correct, all columns and rows will add to the same number.

A. TUTOR
B. MAGWITCH
C. ESTELLA
D. BARGEMEN
E. BLACKSMITH
F. MOLLY
G. STARTOP
H. HERBERT
I. GRAVEYARD
J. WOPSLE
K. HAND
L. FIRE
M. EXPECTATIONS
N. CLARA
O. BRAG
P. MRS JOE

1. Herbert's girlfriend, later his wife
2. Helped Pip and Herbert; former roommate
3. It burned Miss H and Pip
4. Matthew Pocket to Pip; educator
5. Pip and Joe were 'Brought up by ____'
6. Pip's benefactor
7. Great _____
8. The 'pale young gentleman'; Pip's flatmate
9. Joe's occupation
10. Pip's sister
11. Miss Havisham's adopted daughter
12. Church clerk turned actor
13. Three Jolly _____
14. Pip meets a convict there
15. Estella's mother; Jagger's servant
16. '_____ is a good dog, but Holdfast is a better.'

A=4	B=6	C=11	D=13
E=9	F=15	G=2	H=8
I=14	J=12	K=5	L=3
M=7	N=1	O=16	P=10

Great Expectations Magic Squares 2

Match the definition with the vocabulary word. Put your answers in the magic squares below. When your answers are correct, all columns and rows will add to the same number.

A. TUTOR
B. JAGGERS
C. HERBERT
D. WOPSLE
E. LONDON
F. HAND
G. MOLLY
H. PIP
I. MRS JOE
J. HAVISHAM
K. AGED P
L. GREAT
M. DICKENS
N. BLACKSMITH
O. FIRE
P. JOE

1. He has great expectations
2. Matthew Pocket to Pip; educator
3. Pip's guardian
4. Estella's mother; Jagger's servant
5. Spinster woman who uses Pip
6. It burned Miss H and Pip
7. Pip's blacksmith brother-in-law
8. Pip's sister
9. Wemmick's father
10. Joe's occupation
11. Author
12. ____ Expectations
13. Jaggers's office is in this city
14. Church clerk turned actor
15. The 'pale young gentleman'; Pip's flatmate
16. Pip and Joe were 'Brought up by ____'

A=	B=	C=	D=
E=	F=	G=	H=
I=	J=	K=	L=
M=	N=	O=	P=

Great Expectations Magic Squares 2 Answer Key

Match the definition with the vocabulary word. Put your answers in the magic squares below. When your answers are correct, all columns and rows will add to the same number.

A. TUTOR
B. JAGGERS
C. HERBERT
D. WOPSLE
E. LONDON
F. HAND
G. MOLLY
H. PIP
I. MRS JOE
J. HAVISHAM
K. AGED P
L. GREAT
M. DICKENS
N. BLACKSMITH
O. FIRE
P. JOE

1. He has great expectations
2. Matthew Pocket to Pip; educator
3. Pip's guardian
4. Estella's mother; Jagger's servant
5. Spinster woman who uses Pip
6. It burned Miss H and Pip
7. Pip's blacksmith brother-in-law
8. Pip's sister
9. Wemmick's father
10. Joe's occupation
11. Author
12. ____ Expectations
13. Jaggers's office is in this city
14. Church clerk turned actor
15. The 'pale young gentleman'; Pip's flatmate
16. Pip and Joe were 'Brought up by ____'

A=2	B=3	C=15	D=14
E=13	F=16	G=4	H=1
I=8	J=5	K=9	L=12
M=11	N=10	O=6	P=7

Great Expectations Magic Squares 3

Match the definition with the vocabulary word. Put your answers in the magic squares below. When your answers are correct, all columns and rows will add to the same number.

A. HAND
B. WOPSLE
C. TRABB
D. PROVIS
E. JOE
F. ESTELLA
G. EXPECTATIONS
H. BRAG
I. WEMMICK
J. HAVISHAM
K. STARTOP
L. HERBERT
M. DICKENS
N. AGED P
O. GRAVEYARD
P. PUMBLECHOOK

1. Church clerk turned actor
2. Great _____
3. Helped Pip and Herbert; former roommate
4. Wemmick's father
5. Author
6. The 'pale young gentleman'; Pip's flatmate
7. '_____ is a good dog, but Holdfast is a better.'
8. Pip and Joe were 'Brought up by ____'
9. Claimed to be the founder of Pip's fortunes
10. Jaggers's clerk
11. Pip's blacksmith brother-in-law
12. Magwitch's assumed name
13. The letter from ___ & Co. brought news of Mrs. Joe's death
14. Miss Havisham's adopted daughter
15. Spinster woman who uses Pip
16. Pip meets a convict there

A=	B=	C=	D=
E=	F=	G=	H=
I=	J=	K=	L=
M=	N=	O=	P=

Great Expectations Magic Squares 3 Answer Key

Match the definition with the vocabulary word. Put your answers in the magic squares below. When your answers are correct, all columns and rows will add to the same number.

A. HAND
B. WOPSLE
C. TRABB
D. PROVIS
E. JOE
F. ESTELLA
G. EXPECTATIONS
H. BRAG
I. WEMMICK
J. HAVISHAM
K. STARTOP
L. HERBERT
M. DICKENS
N. AGED P
O. GRAVEYARD
P. PUMBLECHOOK

1. Church clerk turned actor
2. Great _____
3. Helped Pip and Herbert; former roommate
4. Wemmick's father
5. Author
6. The 'pale young gentleman'; Pip's flatmate
7. '_____ is a good dog, but Holdfast is a better.'
8. Pip and Joe were 'Brought up by ____'
9. Claimed to be the founder of Pip's fortunes
10. Jaggers's clerk
11. Pip's blacksmith brother-in-law
12. Magwitch's assumed name
13. The letter from ___ & Co. brought news of Mrs. Joe's death
14. Miss Havisham's adopted daughter
15. Spinster woman who uses Pip
16. Pip meets a convict there

A=8	B=1	C=13	D=12
E=11	F=14	G=2	H=7
I=10	J=15	K=3	L=6
M=5	N=4	O=16	P=9

Great Expectations Magic Squares 4

Match the definition with the vocabulary word. Put your answers in the magic squares below. When your answers are correct, all columns and rows will add to the same number.

A. LONDON
B. TRABB
C. PIE
D. DICKENS
E. WOPSLE
F. BIRTHDAY
G. CLOTHES
H. PUMBLECHOOK
I. DRUMMLE
J. GREAT
K. AGED P
L. PIP
M. STARTOP
N. BIDDY
O. GRAVY
P. GRAVEYARD

1. Jaggers's office is in this city
2. Pip's confidant at the Gargery's
3. ____ Expectations
4. Church clerk turned actor
5. 'I'm all wrong in these ____.' (Joe said to Pip)
6. He has great expectations
7. Pip meets a convict there
8. Pip took pork ___ to give to the convict
9. Joe gives Pip extra ___ at dinner with Mr. P
10. Author
11. Claimed to be the founder of Pip's fortunes
12. Wemmick's father
13. Marries Estella
14. Camilla, Raymond & Sara visit Miss H on this day every year
15. The letter from ___ & Co. brought news of Mrs. Joe's death
16. Helped Pip and Herbert; former roommate

A=	B=	C=	D=
E=	F=	G=	H=
I=	J=	K=	L=
M=	N=	O=	P=

Great Expectations Magic Squares 4 Answer Key

Match the definition with the vocabulary word. Put your answers in the magic squares below. When your answers are correct, all columns and rows will add to the same number.

A. LONDON
B. TRABB
C. PIE
D. DICKENS
E. WOPSLE
F. BIRTHDAY
G. CLOTHES
H. PUMBLECHOOK
I. DRUMMLE
J. GREAT
K. AGED P
L. PIP
M. STARTOP
N. BIDDY
O. GRAVY
P. GRAVEYARD

1. Jaggers's office is in this city
2. Pip's confidant at the Gargery's
3. ____ Expectations
4. Church clerk turned actor
5. 'I'm all wrong in these ____.' (Joe said to Pip)
6. He has great expectations
7. Pip meets a convict there
8. Pip took pork ____ to give to the convict
9. Joe gives Pip extra ____ at dinner with Mr. P
10. Author
11. Claimed to be the founder of Pip's fortunes
12. Wemmick's father
13. Marries Estella
14. Camilla, Raymond & Sara visit Miss H on this day every year
15. The letter from ____ & Co. brought news of Mrs. Joe's death
16. Helped Pip and Herbert; former roommate

A=1	B=15	C=8	D=10
E=4	F=14	G=5	H=11
I=13	J=3	K=12	L=6
M=16	N=2	O=9	P=7

Great Expectations Word Search 1

```
H S R C H E O B I R T H D A Y Z T H K J
X J R S H Y X R D Y B J R W Z Y U Z M F
G Z C D H N M P L S D F G J M W T R C T
M N L Z T M S V E I G G G N S P O C P M
G Y T B I K S K P C C M J M Z Z R W Z K
R B R N M F J L D K T K X R R B D S B Z
Y B P P S D F Z G R M A D D P W D K S X
P R K Z K W J W A P Z B T S M G S E D J
G K J D C X P X R D U P X I A C H N R F
R T V C A Y B I G R V M K R O T G A N R
E S T E L L A S E R I F B L O N D O N Q
A Z R L B A N T R K T I W L O V S W G D
T P O T C E R P Y Z D T C I E Y M C R G
J J J C K O Z A T D S W T J E C A W A B
A B M C P H S P Y Y J I P P T K H Z V T
G G I R M T D T L Q S O M M R V S O Y C
G D R R S E R L A O J O E W E O I G O K
E M R A G J O A P R C H O D B R V N Q K
R D F A V M O D B X T P I P R W A I X T
S Y Z T L E J E W B S O F N E U H Z S T
L W T S K R Y W D L Q J P J H M M G Y L
P K F W J B T A E M Y C R J T J D M Z N
B A R G E M E N R E G N E V A J J M L S
M A G W I T C H T D W E M M I C K F N E
```

'I'm all wrong in these ____.' (Joe said to Pip) (7)

'____ is a good dog, but Holdfast is a better.' (4)

Author (7)

Camilla, Raymond & Sara visit Miss H on this day every year (8)

Church clerk turned actor (6)

Claimed to be the founder of Pip's fortunes (11)

Enemy of Magwitch; jilted Miss H (9)

Estella's mother; Jagger's servant (5)

Great _____ (12)

He has great expectations (3)

Helped Pip and Herbert; former roommate (7)

Herbert's girlfriend, later his wife (5)

It burned Miss H and Pip (4)

Jaggers's clerk (7)

Jaggers's office is in this city (6)

Joe gives Pip extra ___ at dinner with Mr. P (5)

Joe's last name (7)

Joe's occupation (10)

Magwitch's assumed name (6)

Marries Estella (7)

Matthew Pocket to Pip; educator (5)

Miss Havisham's adopted daughter (7)

Orlick's position at Miss H's house (6)

Pip and Joe were 'Brought up by ____' (4)

Pip bought one for Herbert so he would have a steady income (8)

Pip meets a convict there (9)

Pip took pork ___ to give to the convict (3)

Pip's benefactor (8)

Pip's blacksmith brother-in-law (3)

Pip's confidant at the Gargery's (5)

Pip's guardian (7)

Pip's servant (7)

Pip's sister (6)

Spinster woman who uses Pip (8)

The 'pale young gentleman'; Pip's flatmate (7)

The letter from ___ & Co. brought news of Mrs. Joe's death (5)

Three Jolly _____ (8)

Three _____ Bargemen (5)

Tries to kill Pip (6)

Wemmick's father (5)

____ Expectations (5)

Great Expectations Word Search 1 Answer Key

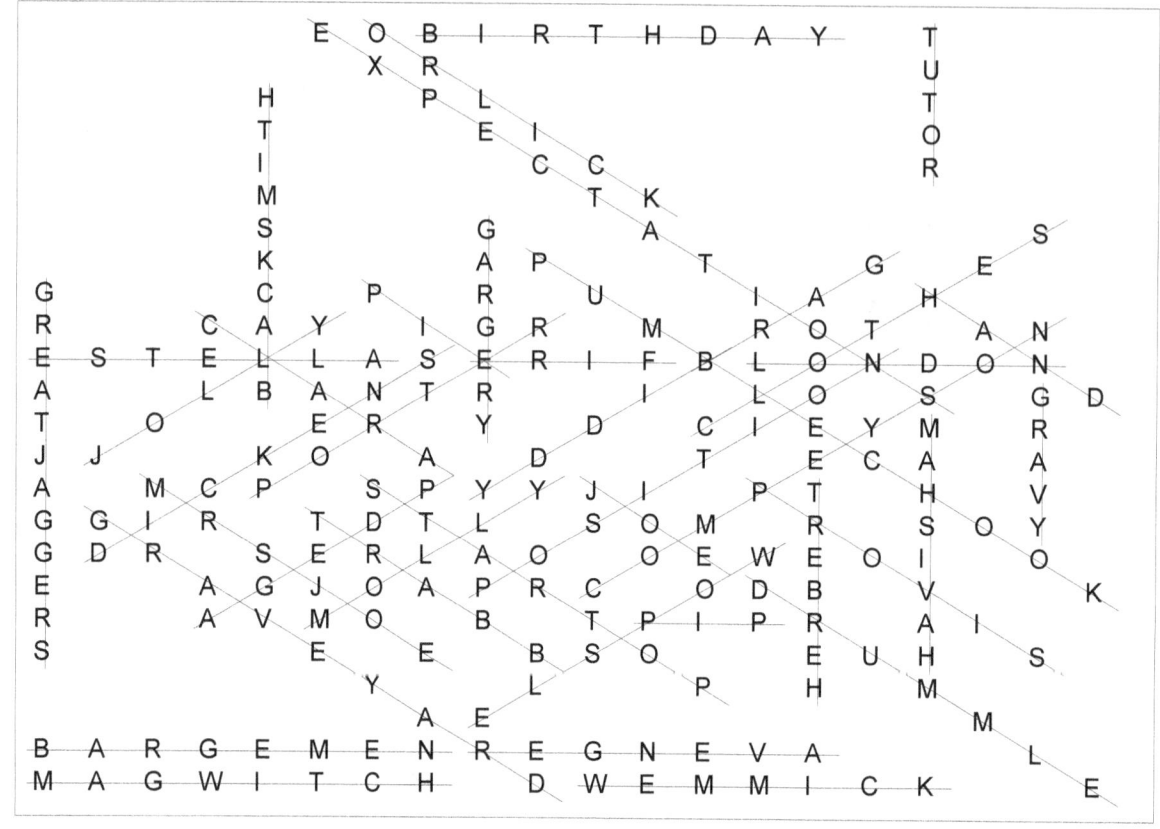

'I'm all wrong in these ____.' (Joe said to Pip) (7)

'____ is a good dog, but Holdfast is a better.' (4)

Author (7)

Camilla, Raymond & Sara visit Miss H on this day every year (8)

Church clerk turned actor (6)

Claimed to be the founder of Pip's fortunes (11)

Enemy of Magwitch; jilted Miss H (9)

Estella's mother; Jagger's servant (5)

Great _____ (12)

He has great expectations (3)

Helped Pip and Herbert; former roommate (7)

Herbert's girlfriend, later his wife (5)

It burned Miss H and Pip (4)

Jaggers's clerk (7)

Jaggers's office is in this city (6)

Joe gives Pip extra ___ at dinner with Mr. P (5)

Joe's last name (7)

Joe's occupation (10)

Magwitch's assumed name (6)

Marries Estella (7)

Matthew Pocket to Pip; educator (5)

Miss Havisham's adopted daughter (7)

Orlick's position at Miss H's house (6)

Pip and Joe were 'Brought up by ____' (4)

Pip bought one for Herbert so he would have a steady income (8)

Pip meets a convict there (9)

Pip took pork ___ to give to the convict (3)

Pip's benefactor (8)

Pip's blacksmith brother-in-law (3)

Pip's confidant at the Gargery's (5)

Pip's guardian (7)

Pip's servant (7)

Pip's sister (6)

Spinster woman who uses Pip (8)

The 'pale young gentleman'; Pip's flatmate (7)

The letter from ___ & Co. brought news of Mrs. Joe's death (5)

Three Jolly _____ (8)

Three _____ Bargemen (5)

Tries to kill Pip (6)

Wemmick's father (5)

____ Expectations (5)

Great Expectations Word Search 2

```
L M R S J O E L M Y C O M P E Y S O N P
O N W P J S K C A P H W V V K E G E F Z
N G R V C T R D L X L Q J K H K W X T K
D K R B F W H G D X D F Y T N K C P P D
O K Q Y H T X R J N Q V O S X M X E L X
N F H C R P W P V Q D L Z N B L B C J D
T V C I L D K O O H C E L B M U P T Q W
N C B C Y R M L H J C J Y D W R T A J M
W J X D F A X D C B Y X R S K X B T C P
T B P L F Y T S I S G T Z K R K P I B V
G R T T G E L R M C P D U B R C R O I Z
A R A C A V P S S G K M H T J I O N D L
R H N B R A I R T R M E A H O L V S D Q
G T R E B R E H M A V E N G E R I F Y D
E I M M B G C S H V R E D S E O S L P Y
R M W H G T Q S T Y M T W G H D L B I S
Y S D A I G I P D E Y W O Q R O P N P Y
W K J W W V J O G W L C O P M E Q O D K
E C G D A N S R D Q L L Y P N C A I R X
M A T H R J A T J D O A A G S S X T U L
M L K P B B M E B G J R G X J L X I M L
I B T K L L G R Z Z S A P T X V E S M Y
C P F F Q F L D M S J J T L D L C O L S
K C C J V X C R Y W N L R T Q K V P E Z
```

'I'm all wrong in these ____.' (Joe said to Pip) (7)
'____ is a good dog, but Holdfast is a better.' (4)
Author (7)
Camilla, Raymond & Sara visit Miss H on this day every year (8)
Church clerk turned actor (6)
Claimed to be the founder of Pip's fortunes (11)
Enemy of Magwitch; jilted Miss H (9)
Estella's mother; Jagger's servant (5)
Great _____ (12)
He has great expectations (3)
Helped Pip and Herbert; former roommate (7)
Herbert's girlfriend, later his wife (5)
It burned Miss H and Pip (4)
Jaggers's clerk (7)
Jaggers's office is in this city (6)
Joe gives Pip extra ___ at dinner with Mr. P (5)
Joe's last name (7)
Joe's occupation (10)
Magwitch's assumed name (6)
Marries Estella (7)
Matthew Pocket to Pip; educator (5)
Miss Havisham's adopted daughter (7)
Orlick's position at Miss H's house (6)
Pip and Joe were 'Brought up by ____' (4)
Pip bought one for Herbert so he would have a steady income (8)
Pip meets a convict there (9)
Pip took pork ___ to give to the convict (3)
Pip's benefactor (8)
Pip's blacksmith brother-in-law (3)
Pip's confidant at the Gargery's (5)
Pip's guardian (7)
Pip's servant (7)
Pip's sister (6)
Spinster woman who uses Pip (8)
The 'pale young gentleman'; Pip's flatmate (7)
The letter from ___ & Co. brought news of Mrs. Joe's death (5)
Three Jolly _____ (8)
Three _____ Bargemen (5)
Tries to kill Pip (6)
Wemmick's father (5)
____ Expectations (5)

Great Expectations Word Search 2 Answer Key

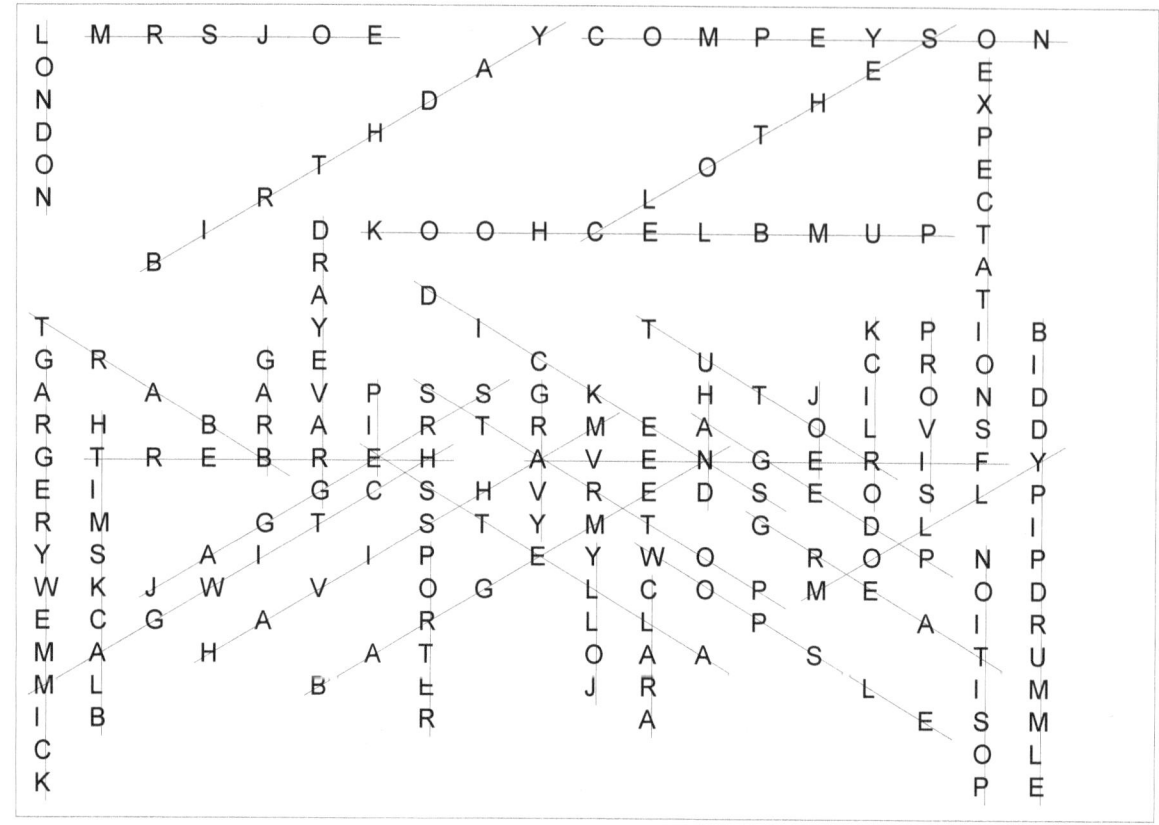

'I'm all wrong in these ____.' (Joe said to Pip) (7)
'_____ is a good dog, but Holdfast is a better.' (4)
Author (7)
Camilla, Raymond & Sara visit Miss H on this day every year (8)
Church clerk turned actor (6)
Claimed to be the founder of Pip's fortunes (11)
Enemy of Magwitch; jilted Miss H (9)
Estella's mother; Jagger's servant (5)
Great _____ (12)
He has great expectations (3)
Helped Pip and Herbert; former roommate (7)
Herbert's girlfriend, later his wife (5)
It burned Miss H and Pip (4)
Jaggers's clerk (7)
Jaggers's office is in this city (6)
Joe gives Pip extra ___ at dinner with Mr. P (5)
Joe's last name (7)
Joe's occupation (10)
Magwitch's assumed name (6)
Marries Estella (7)
Matthew Pocket to Pip; educator (5)
Miss Havisham's adopted daughter (7)
Orlick's position at Miss H's house (6)
Pip and Joe were 'Brought up by ____' (4)
Pip bought one for Herbert so he would have a steady income (8)
Pip meets a convict there (9)
Pip took pork ___ to give to the convict (3)
Pip's benefactor (8)
Pip's blacksmith brother-in-law (3)
Pip's confidant at the Gargery's (5)
Pip's guardian (7)
Pip's servant (7)
Pip's sister (6)
Spinster woman who uses Pip (8)
The 'pale young gentleman'; Pip's flatmate (7)
The letter from ___ & Co. brought news of Mrs. Joe's death (5)
Three Jolly _____ (8)
Three _____ Bargemen (5)
Tries to kill Pip (6)
Wemmick's father (5)
____ Expectations (5)

Great Expectations Word Search 3

```
T P X W Y H B D Y E X P E C T A T I O N S G S T Z
L Y F W Y Q V A P X G H G H K X Q P W H W H J R P
X K P R Y Z D M X W X N B W X R T G J T M Y W J D
N H D H J H F M Y V H Z L H Z S V J Y W N F W L V
H B G D T T C T H Y R P A M M M J P B W X J R G V
A R M R W Z J J K Y W V C R C O L A E T X L L A Y
V T I V O N Z T S C N Z K Q Y R T M G M T D L R H
I B B R P N L F M T R M S T J L M J S G O L F G P
S F A B S C I J C K A N M D K I D N W B E L H E M
H H F V L R F O M L Q R I T C C E B A H P R L R M
A W G R E A T L B B A R T K U K M R S J O E S Y X
M G K L C N M L R C J R H O C T G A M B O F T J H
G C E Y W W G Y J T E P A I P E O G X T Q E S N N
G H L D T D Y E N B J L D S M H N R W P G R G B N
P I E O P P I P R V I W W E C O M P E Y S O N N X
O O G Q T F Q E N M J D N S N P P V K X B C P H B
S J R R V H H P Q L A J D D R J J M N H B F R S D
I K M T A W E H A N D G R Y P U M B L E C H O O K
T J S B E V W S L Q D A W W L C B J K S G W V R B
I G X P T R Y S W L Y R T I R X G D P T J N I J G
O L O N D O N X M E X S U T T D W Q Z E S K S N M
N J P N T T G V V H T G C M M C J R Y L C F D X M
P Q L M W W Y A T G D L H T M C H C C L Y Y D N L
R X W V T D R B Y R R M L Y Z L N M D A V C G Z L
K R S M K G V L R Q W L R F G F E V G H G P K T T
```

AGEDP	COMPEYSON	GREAT	MOLLY	STARTOP
AVENGER	DICKENS	HAND	MRSJOE	TRABB
BARGEMEN	DRUMMLE	HAVISHAM	ORLICK	TUTOR
BIDDY	ESTELLA	HERBERT	PIE	WEMMICK
BIRTHDAY	EXPECTATIONS	JAGGERS	PIP	WOPSLE
BLACKSMITH	FIRE	JOE	PORTER	
BRAG	GARGERY	JOLLY	POSITION	
CLARA	GRAVEYARD	LONDON	PROVIS	
CLOTHES	GRAVY	MAGWITCH	PUMBLECHOOK	

Great Expectations Word Search 3 Answer Key

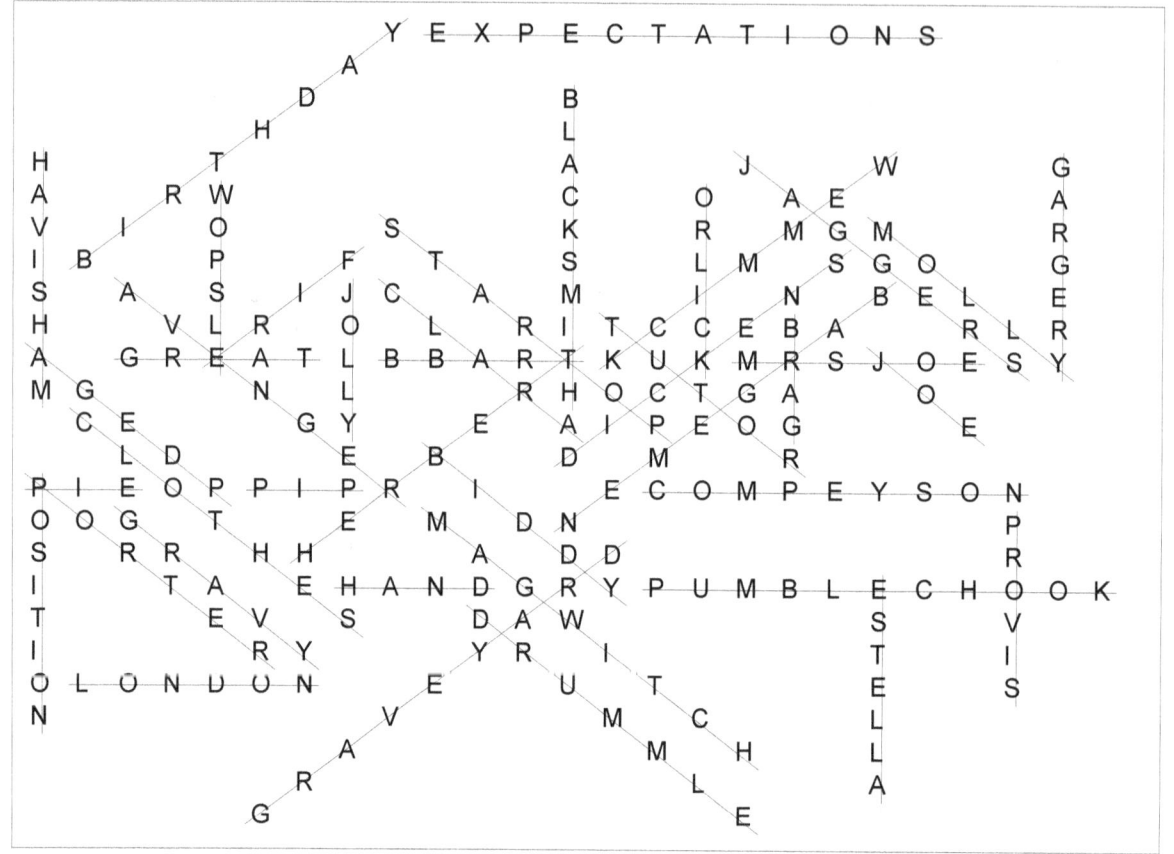

AGEDP	COMPEYSON	GREAT	MOLLY	STARTOP
AVENGER	DICKENS	HAND	MRSJOE	TRABB
BARGEMEN	DRUMMLE	HAVISHAM	ORLICK	TUTOR
BIDDY	ESTELLA	HERBERT	PIE	WEMMICK
BIRTHDAY	EXPECTATIONS	JAGGERS	PIP	WOPSLE
BLACKSMITH	FIRE	JOE	PORTER	
BRAG	GARGERY	JOLLY	POSITION	
CLARA	GRAVEYARD	LONDON	PROVIS	
CLOTHES	GRAVY	MAGWITCH	PUMBLECHOOK	

Great Expectations Word Search 4

```
C O M P E Y S O N N E H D B D T J D V S S E T P N
F S X L L J N L P L T W M I W Y N H W F T X W U Z
Y G Q W H J Q R S I R F T H C J Q S Q S T P H M Q
B V J Z Y V T P M B K Q F Y P K Z Y D Z P E Y B B
Z Q L H W J O S J P N W D M M F E Y V Q Z C P L Q
C N F Z G W K R F S K K R S B G B N J L C T P E H
B H X Q D C Y Y Y M V P C P B R P D S B K A T C B
W B V X A X L C K J S G T R N F K W X J R T Q H C
V N Z L S S M B W T N V H N K W B D J W H I P O H
P B B Q J K C Y D G F B D P X H F V P W R O F O Y
J D X Z W W K Q F C N A B R N V A W G S R N Y K M
P Y K X Y C Z K V M V T S I M P C V E B C S T P P
R O D W Q T G M R E F B Z F R L Z Q I M P Y R T M
B G R C H U L S N C S A T X O T C B T S M N H T R
D D B T L T G G F G Y R V T H X H T J P H I T C E
R Z X R E O E R N R T G H G M P T D J G Q A C L J
H E R B E R T W E S T E L L A R X S A P I P M K N
G S H K H Q J G R A S M V X A O S R Z Y H M O C N
B S S D R Z R B I R T E H B R V B J J S U J L L M
K T N C Y A D Z F M C N B E B I L V O R Z O L A L
N A M A G W I T C H N O I T I S O P D E H L Y R G
H R G G J F J K Q Y V P Z S D Z N L O G S L Z A J
B T M E X R W Y G S K B X D Y D J K G W Y V N R R
Q O M D D R A Y E V A R G X Y Y O G R A V Y M H N
B P V J T P O R L I C K M N P K N J R J L C V J Z
```

AGEDP	COMPEYSON	GREAT	MOLLY	STARTOP
AVENGER	DICKENS	HAND	MRSJOE	TRABB
BARGEMEN	DRUMMLE	HAVISHAM	ORLICK	TUTOR
BIDDY	ESTELLA	HERBERT	PIE	WEMMICK
BIRTHDAY	EXPECTATIONS	JAGGERS	PIP	WOPSLE
BLACKSMITH	FIRE	JOE	PORTER	
BRAG	GARGERY	JOLLY	POSITION	
CLARA	GRAVEYARD	LONDON	PROVIS	
CLOTHES	GRAVY	MAGWITCH	PUMBLECHOOK	

Great Expectations Word Search 4 Answer Key

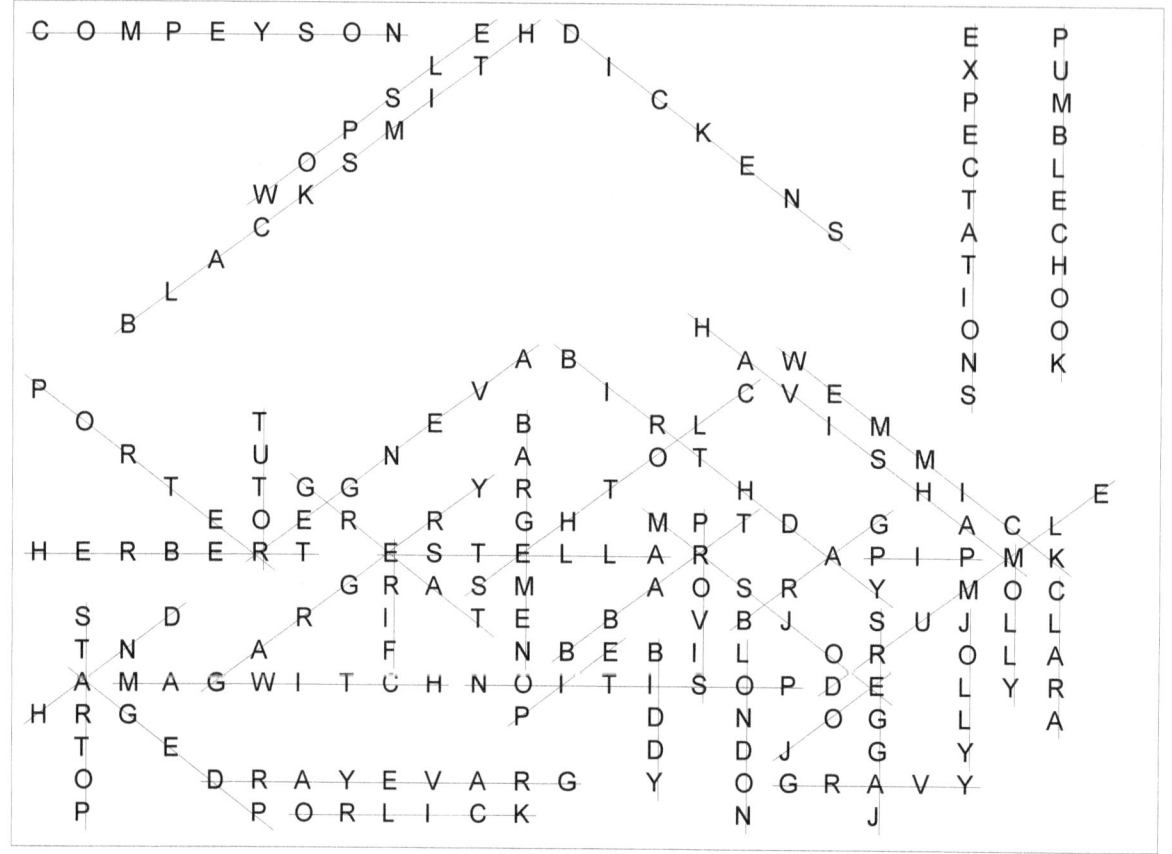

AGEDP	COMPEYSON	GREAT	MOLLY	STARTOP
AVENGER	DICKENS	HAND	MRSJOE	TRABB
BARGEMEN	DRUMMLE	HAVISHAM	ORLICK	TUTOR
BIDDY	ESTELLA	HERBERT	PIE	WEMMICK
BIRTHDAY	EXPECTATIONS	JAGGERS	PIP	WOPSLE
BLACKSMITH	FIRE	JOE	PORTER	
BRAG	GARGERY	JOLLY	POSITION	
CLARA	GRAVEYARD	LONDON	PROVIS	
CLOTHES	GRAVY	MAGWITCH	PUMBLECHOOK	

Great Expectations Crossword 1

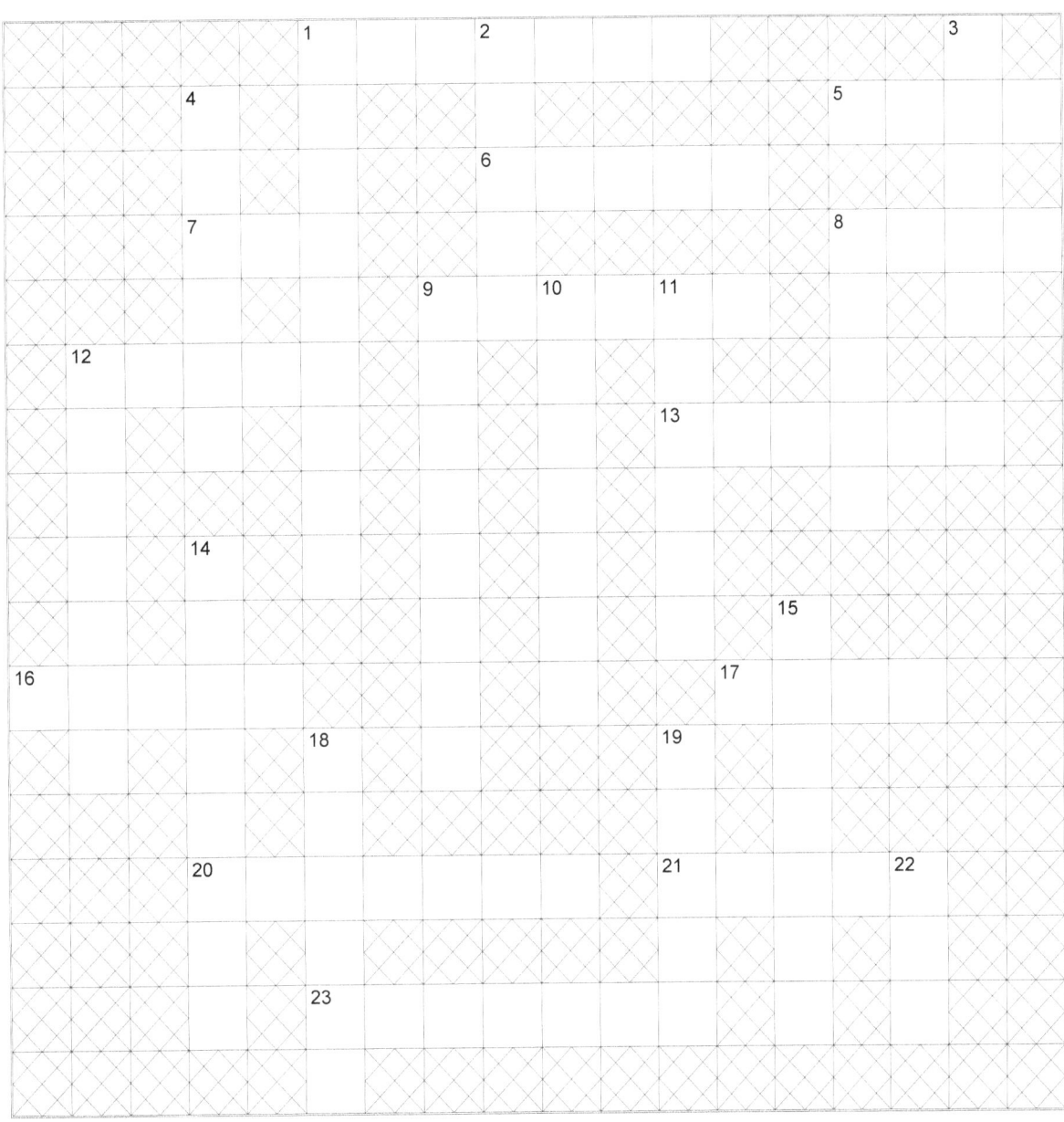

Across
1. 'I'm all wrong in these ____.' (Joe said to Pip)
5. It burned Miss H and Pip
6. The letter from ___ & Co. brought news of Mrs. Joe's death
7. He has great expectations
8. '____ is a good dog, but Holdfast is a better.'
9. Pip's sister
12. Three _____ Bargemen
13. Jaggers's office is in this city
16. Joe gives Pip extra ___ at dinner with Mr. P
17. Pip and Joe were 'Brought up by ____'
20. The 'pale young gentleman'; Pip's flatmate
21. Wemmick's father
23. Miss Havisham's adopted daughter

Down
1. Enemy of Magwitch; jilted Miss H
2. Matthew Pocket to Pip; educator
3. ____ Expectations
4. Church clerk turned actor
8. Pip's confidant at the Gargery's
9. Pip's benefactor
10. Helped Pip and Herbert; former roommate
11. Tries to kill Pip
12. Pip's guardian
14. Spinster woman who uses Pip
15. Joe's last name
18. Orlick's position at Miss H's house
19. Herbert's girlfriend, later his wife
22. Pip took pork ___ to give to the convict

Great Expectations Crossword 1 Answer Key

					1		2					3	
					C	L	O	T	H	E	S	G	
			4		O					5			
			W		O		U			F	I	R	E
			O		M		6						
			O		M		T	R	A	B	B	E	
			7				O			8			
			P	I	P		O			B	R	A	G
			S		E	9	10		11				
			S		E	M	R	S	J	O	E	T	
	12												
	J	O	L	L	Y	A	T		R	D			
								13					
	A		E		S	G	A	L	O	N	D	O	N
	G				O	W	R	I	Y				
			14										
	G		H		N	I	T	C					
	E		A		T	O	K	15					
								G					
16								17					
G	R	A	V	Y	C	P	H	A	N	D			
	S			18			19						
	S		I	P	H		C	R					
				O			L	G					
			20				21			22			
			H	E	R	B	E	R	T	A	G	E	D	P
			A	T				R		R		I	
			M	23									
			M	E	S	T	E	L	L	A	Y	E	
				R									

Across
1. 'I'm all wrong in these ____.' (Joe said to Pip)
5. It burned Miss H and Pip
6. The letter from ___ & Co. brought news of Mrs. Joe's death
7. He has great expectations
8. '____ is a good dog, but Holdfast is a better.'
9. Pip's sister
12. Three _____ Bargemen
13. Jaggers's office is in this city
16. Joe gives Pip extra ___ at dinner with Mr. P
17. Pip and Joe were 'Brought up by ____'
20. The 'pale young gentleman'; Pip's flatmate
21. Wemmick's father
23. Miss Havisham's adopted daughter

Down
1. Enemy of Magwitch; jilted Miss H
2. Matthew Pocket to Pip; educator
3. ____ Expectations
4. Church clerk turned actor
8. Pip's confidant at the Gargery's
9. Pip's benefactor
10. Helped Pip and Herbert; former roommate
11. Tries to kill Pip
12. Pip's guardian
14. Spinster woman who uses Pip
15. Joe's last name
18. Orlick's position at Miss H's house
19. Herbert's girlfriend, later his wife
22. Pip took pork ___ to give to the convict

Great Expectations Crossword 2

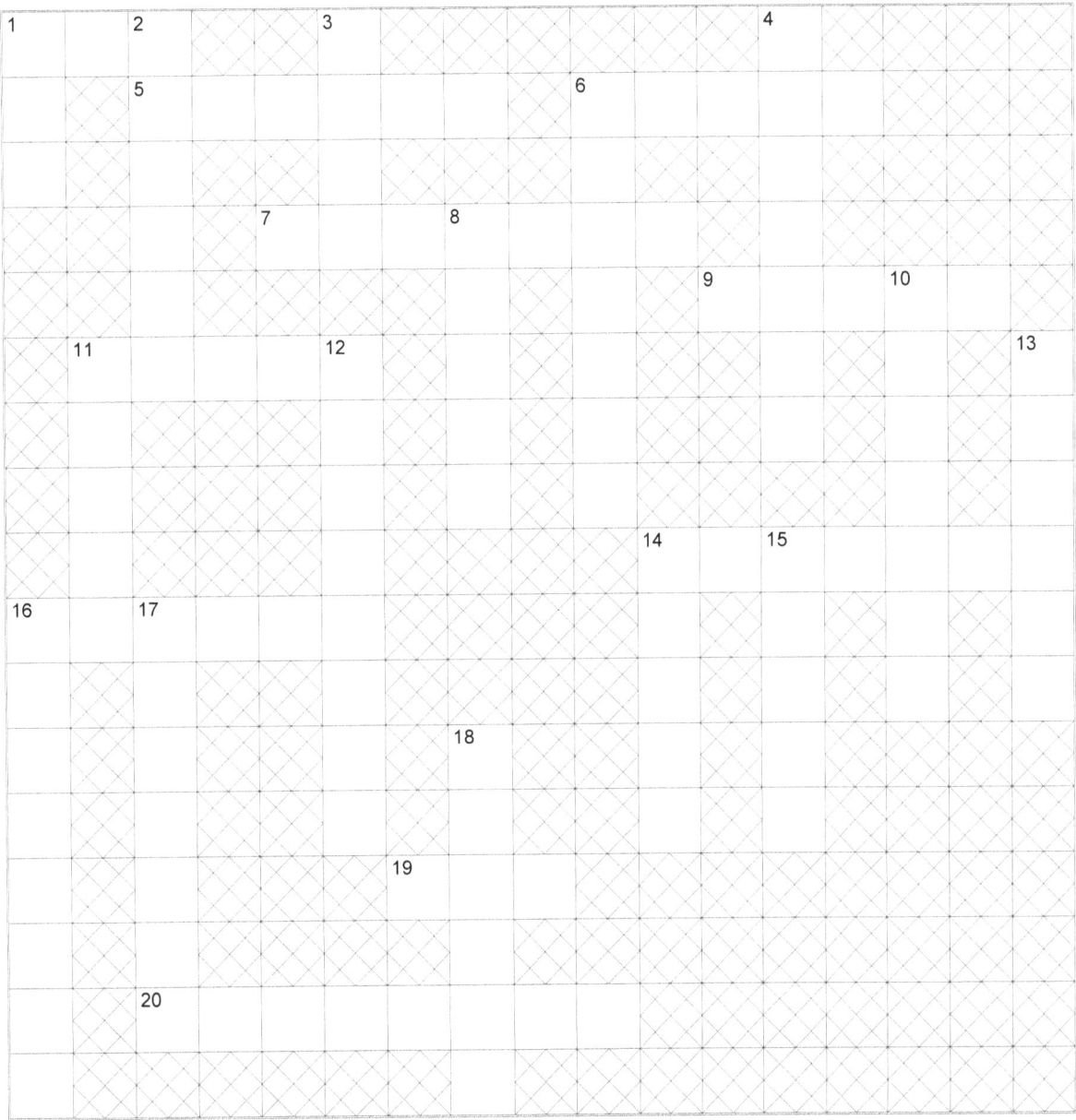

Across
1. He has great expectations
5. Tries to kill Pip
6. Joe gives Pip extra ___ at dinner with Mr. P
7. The 'pale young gentleman'; Pip's flatmate
9. Wemmick's father
11. The letter from ___ & Co. brought news of Mrs. Joe's death
14. Pip's guardian
16. Pip's sister
19. Pip's blacksmith brother-in-law
20. Pip bought one for Herbert so he would have a steady income

Down
1. Pip took pork ___ to give to the convict
2. Orlick's position at Miss H's house
3. It burned Miss H and Pip
4. Pip's servant
6. Joe's last name
8. Pip's confidant at the Gargery's
10. Author
11. Matthew Pocket to Pip; educator
12. Three Jolly _____
13. Church clerk turned actor
14. Three _____ Bargemen
15. ___ Expectations
16. Pip's benefactor
17. Helped Pip and Herbert; former roommate
18. Magwitch's assumed name

Great Expectations Crossword 2 Answer Key

¹P	I	²P			³F				⁴A			
I		⁵O	R	L	I	C	K		⁶G	R	A	V	Y
E		R			R				A			E	
		T		⁷H	E	R	⁸B	E	R	T		N	
		E			I		G			⁹A	G	E	¹⁰D	P
	¹¹T	R	A	B	¹²B		D		E		E		I	¹³W
	U				A		D		R		R		C	O
	T				R		Y		Y				K	P
	O				G					¹⁴J	A	G	G	¹⁵E	R	S
¹⁶M	¹⁷S	J	O	E					O		R		N		L
A	T			M					L		E		S		E
G	A			E			¹⁸P		L		A				
W	R			N			R		Y		T				
I	T				¹⁹J	O	E								
T	O				V										
C	²⁰P	O	S	I	T	I	O	N							
H					S										

Across
1. He has great expectations
5. Tries to kill Pip
6. Joe gives Pip extra ___ at dinner with Mr. P
7. The 'pale young gentleman'; Pip's flatmate
9. Wemmick's father
11. The letter from ___ & Co. brought news of Mrs. Joe's death
14. Pip's guardian
16. Pip's sister
19. Pip's blacksmith brother-in-law
20. Pip bought one for Herbert so he would have a steady income

Down
1. Pip took pork ___ to give to the convict
2. Orlick's position at Miss H's house
3. It burned Miss H and Pip
4. Pip's servant
6. Joe's last name
8. Pip's confidant at the Gargery's
10. Author
11. Matthew Pocket to Pip; educator
12. Three Jolly _____
13. Church clerk turned actor
14. Three _____ Bargemen
15. ____ Expectations
16. Pip's benefactor
17. Helped Pip and Herbert; former roommate
18. Magwitch's assumed name

Great Expectations Crossword 3

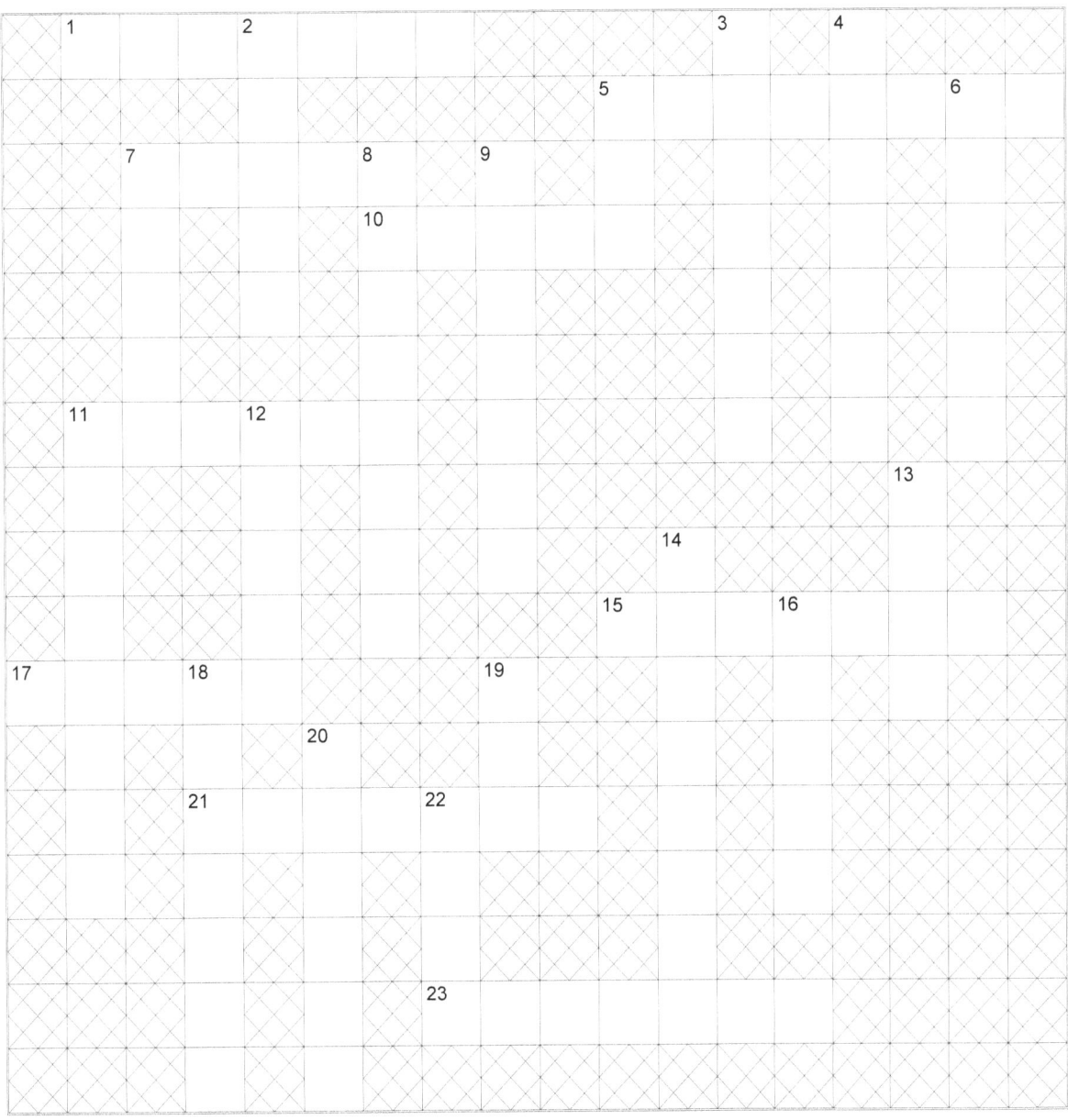

Across
1. Pip's guardian
5. Pip bought one for Herbert so he would have a steady income
7. The letter from ___ & Co. brought news of Mrs. Joe's death
10. Wemmick's father
11. Pip's sister
15. Joe's last name
17. Pip's confidant at the Gargery's
21. 'I'm all wrong in these ____.' (Joe said to Pip)
23. Marries Estella

Down
2. Joe gives Pip extra ___ at dinner with Mr. P
3. Miss Havisham's adopted daughter
4. Helped Pip and Herbert; former roommate
5. He has great expectations
6. Tries to kill Pip
7. Matthew Pocket to Pip; educator
8. Three Jolly _____
9. The 'pale young gentleman'; Pip's flatmate
11. Pip's benefactor
12. Three _____ Bargemen
13. It burned Miss H and Pip
14. Spinster woman who uses Pip
16. ____ Expectations
18. Author
19. Pip's blacksmith brother-in-law
20. Church clerk turned actor
22. Pip and Joe were 'Brought up by ____'

Great Expectations Crossword 3 Answer Key

	1 J	A	G	2 G	E	R	S			3 E		4 S		
				R					5 P	O	S	I	T	I	O	N
		7 T	R	A	B	8 B		9 H		I		T	A		R
			U		V		10 A	G	E	D	P		E	R		L
			T		Y		R		R			L	T		I
			O				G		B			L	O		C
		11 M	R	S	12 J	O	E		E			A	P		K
			A				O		M		R			13 F	
			G				L		E		T	14 H		I	
			W				L		N	15 G	A	16 R	G	E	R	Y
17 B	I	D	18 D	Y				19 J		V		R		E
	T		I		20 W			O		I		E	
	C		21 C	L	O	T	22 H	E	S		S	A	
	H		K		P		A				H	T	
			E		S		N				A		
			N				23 D	R	U	M	M	L	E
			S		E								

Across
1. Pip's guardian
5. Pip bought one for Herbert so he would have a steady income
7. The letter from ___ & Co. brought news of Mrs. Joe's death
10. Wemmick's father
11. Pip's sister
15. Joe's last name
17. Pip's confidant at the Gargery's
21. 'I'm all wrong in these ____.' (Joe said to Pip)
23. Marries Estella

Down
2. Joe gives Pip extra ___ at dinner with Mr. P
3. Miss Havisham's adopted daughter
4. Helped Pip and Herbert; former roommate
5. He has great expectations
6. Tries to kill Pip
7. Matthew Pocket to Pip; educator
8. Three Jolly _____
9. The 'pale young gentleman'; Pip's flatmate
11. Pip's benefactor
12. Three _____ Bargemen
13. It burned Miss H and Pip
14. Spinster woman who uses Pip
16. ____ Expectations
18. Author
19. Pip's blacksmith brother-in-law
20. Church clerk turned actor
22. Pip and Joe were 'Brought up by ____'

Great Expectations Crossword 4

Across
2. Joe gives Pip extra ___ at dinner with Mr. P
4. Tries to kill Pip
7. It burned Miss H and Pip
8. Joe's last name
9. Pip's confidant at the Gargery's
13. Enemy of Magwitch; jilted Miss H
15. Author
17. '___ is a good dog, but Holdfast is a better.'
18. Pip and Joe were 'Brought up by ___'
19. Pip's sister
21. The letter from ___ & Co. brought news of Mrs. Joe's death
22. Miss Havisham's adopted daughter
23. Pip took pork ___ to give to the convict

Down
1. Pip's blacksmith brother-in-law
2. ___ Expectations
3. He has great expectations
5. Jaggers's office is in this city
6. Marries Estella
9. Joe's occupation
10. Camilla, Raymond & Sara visit Miss H on this day every year
11. Wemmick's father
12. 'I'm all wrong in these ___.' (Joe said to Pip)
14. Orlick's position at Miss H's house
16. Church clerk turned actor
20. Helped Pip and Herbert; former roommate
21. Matthew Pocket to Pip; educator

Great Expectations Crossword 4 Answer Key

		1 J						2 G	R	A	V	Y
	3 P	4 O	R	5 L	I	C	K	6 D		R		
7 F	I	R	E	O			8 G	A	R	G	E	R Y
	P			N				U		A		
		9 B	I	D	D	Y		M		T		10 B
11 A		L		O				M		12 C		I
G		A		N				L		L		R
E		C			13 C	O	M	14 P	E	Y	S	O N	T
15 D	I	C	K	E	N	S		O		T		H
P		S		16 W	17 B	R	A	G		10 H	A	N D
		19 M	20 R	S	J	O	E			E		A
		I		T		P		E		S		Y
		T		A		S		21 T	R	A	B	B
		H		R		L		U				
		T		22 E	S	T	E	L	L	A		
		O				O						
		23 P	I	E		R						

Across
2. Joe gives Pip extra ___ at dinner with Mr. P
4. Tries to kill Pip
7. It burned Miss H and Pip
8. Joe's last name
9. Pip's confidant at the Gargery's
13. Enemy of Magwitch; jilted Miss H
15. Author
17. '___ is a good dog, but Holdfast is a better.'
18. Pip and Joe were 'Brought up by ___'
19. Pip's sister
21. The letter from ___ & Co. brought news of Mrs. Joe's death
22. Miss Havisham's adopted daughter
23. Pip took pork ___ to give to the convict

Down
1. Pip's blacksmith brother-in-law
2. ___ Expectations
3. He has great expectations
5. Jaggers's office is in this city
6. Marries Estella
9. Joe's occupation
10. Camilla, Raymond & Sara visit Miss H on this day every year
11. Wemmick's father
12. 'I'm all wrong in these ___.' (Joe said to Pip)
14. Orlick's position at Miss H's house
16. Church clerk turned actor
20. Helped Pip and Herbert; former roommate
21. Matthew Pocket to Pip; educator

Great Expectations

BRAG	MOLLY	WEMMICK	TRABB	MRS JOE
CLOTHES	DICKENS	DRUMMLE	MAGWITCH	POSITION
PIP	PORTER	FREE SPACE	WOPSLE	ORLICK
TUTOR	PIE	STARTOP	GRAVY	JOE
HERBERT	JOLLY	BIRTHDAY	EXPECTATIONS	GARGERY

Great Expectations

BIDDY	BARGEMEN	HAND	AVENGER	PUMBLECHOOK
LONDON	AGED P	FIRE	PROVIS	ESTELLA
CLARA	JAGGERS	FREE SPACE	COMPEYSON	GREAT
BLACKSMITH	GARGERY	EXPECTATIONS	BIRTHDAY	JOLLY
HERBERT	JOE	GRAVY	STARTOP	PIE

Great Expectations

AVENGER	BIDDY	PIE	PORTER	GREAT
FIRE	JOLLY	GRAVEYARD	COMPEYSON	PIP
WEMMICK	CLARA	FREE SPACE	BRAG	WOPSLE
BLACKSMITH	HAVISHAM	PUMBLECHOOK	HAND	PROVIS
CARCERY	MRS JOE	TUTOR	MAGWITCH	BARGEMEN

Great Expectations

TRABB	JAGGERS	LONDON	EXPECTATIONS	JOE
AGED P	BIRTHDAY	ESTELLA	MOLLY	POSITION
ORLICK	DRUMMLE	FREE SPACE	STARTOP	DICKENS
HERBERT	BARGEMEN	MAGWITCH	TUTOR	MRS JOE
GARGERY	PROVIS	HAND	PUMBLECHOOK	HAVISHAM

Great Expectations

PIE	FIRE	MAGWITCH	EXPECTATIONS	GRAVY
PUMBLECHOOK	TRABB	PROVIS	BLACKSMITH	PIP
BRAG	MOLLY	FREE SPACE	DRUMMLE	BARGEMEN
ESTELLA	WEMMICK	MRS JOE	CLOTHES	AGED P
BIDDY	HERBERT	WOPSLE	LONDON	HAND

Great Expectations

JOE	BIRTHDAY	HAVISHAM	COMPEYSON	TUTOR
JAGGERS	PORTER	CLARA	DICKENS	JOLLY
ORLICK	AVENGER	FREE SPACE	POSITION	GREAT
GRAVEYARD	HAND	LONDON	WOPSLE	HERBERT
BIDDY	AGED P	CLOTHES	MRS JOE	WEMMICK

Great Expectations

JOE	GRAVY	BIDDY	AGED P	HERBERT
BRAG	PIE	CLOTHES	TRABB	ORLICK
MRS JOE	WOPSLE	FREE SPACE	BLACKSMITH	DRUMMLE
POSITION	BARGEMEN	LONDON	PIP	PORTER
HAND	WEMMICK	GRAVEYARD	PUMBLECHOOK	FIRE

Great Expectations

PROVIS	GREAT	MAGWITCH	AVENGER	CLARA
MOLLY	EXPECTATIONS	DICKENS	JAGGERS	STARTOP
JOLLY	COMPEYSON	FREE SPACE	ESTELLA	TUTOR
GARGERY	FIRE	PUMBLECHOOK	GRAVEYARD	WEMMICK
HAND	PORTER	PIP	LONDON	BARGEMEN

Great Expectations

LONDON	FIRE	DICKENS	HERBERT	HAVISHAM
AVENGER	BIDDY	GARGERY	CLARA	GRAVEYARD
WOPSLE	PORTER	FREE SPACE	GREAT	STARTOP
MOLLY	BRAG	WEMMICK	EXPECTATIONS	BIRTHDAY
ORLICK	ESTELLA	MRS JOE	BARGEMEN	BLACKSMITH

Great Expectations

POSITION	CLOTHES	JOLLY	JAGGERS	GRAVY
HAND	PIE	TUTOR	PROVIS	PUMBLECHOOK
MAGWITCH	PIP	FREE SPACE	JOE	COMPEYSON
AGED P	BLACKSMITH	BARGEMEN	MRS JOE	ESTELLA
ORLICK	BIRTHDAY	EXPECTATIONS	WEMMICK	BRAG

Great Expectations

DRUMMLE	FIRE	JOE	ESTELLA	DICKENS
GREAT	JAGGERS	ORLICK	HERBERT	LONDON
AGED P	GRAVY	FREE SPACE	POSITION	HAND
GARGERY	STARTOP	BIDDY	HAVISHAM	MOLLY
MRS JOE	JOLLY	EXPECTATIONS	PIE	PORTER

Great Expectations

GRAVEYARD	WEMMICK	AVENGER	BRAG	TRABB
BIRTHDAY	CLOTHES	BARGEMEN	PIP	PROVIS
BLACKSMITH	PUMBLECHOOK	FREE SPACE	COMPEYSON	TUTOR
CLARA	PORTER	PIE	EXPECTATIONS	JOLLY
MRS JOE	MOLLY	HAVISHAM	BIDDY	STARTOP

Great Expectations

ESTELLA	FIRE	POSITION	HAVISHAM	JAGGERS
AGED P	HAND	BIRTHDAY	ORLICK	COMPEYSON
LONDON	GRAVY	FREE SPACE	JOLLY	PROVIS
BARGEMEN	BRAG	CLOTHES	MRS JOE	GARGERY
GRAVEYARD	EXPECTATIONS	WOPSLE	BLACKSMITH	DICKENS

Great Expectations

PIE	MAGWITCH	WEMMICK	HERBERT	CLARA
TRABB	STARTOP	PUMBLECHOOK	PIP	BIDDY
PORTER	AVENGER	FREE SPACE	GREAT	TUTOR
MOLLY	DICKENS	BLACKSMITH	WOPSLE	EXPECTATIONS
GRAVEYARD	GARGERY	MRS JOE	CLOTHES	BRAG

Great Expectations

HERBERT	MAGWITCH	JAGGERS	WEMMICK	POSITION
JOE	AVENGER	GARGERY	MOLLY	WOPSLE
PIE	BRAG	FREE SPACE	AGED P	BLACKSMITH
GRAVEYARD	HAVISHAM	STARTOP	ORLICK	BIRTHDAY
CLARA	HAND	FIRE	CLOTHES	GREAT

Great Expectations

EXPECTATIONS	JOLLY	GRAVY	BIDDY	ESTELLA
PROVIS	LONDON	BARGEMEN	TUTOR	DRUMMLE
DICKENS	COMPEYSON	FREE SPACE	PUMBLECHOOK	PIP
TRABB	GREAT	CLOTHES	FIRE	HAND
CLARA	BIRTHDAY	ORLICK	STARTOP	HAVISHAM

Great Expectations

AGED P	BIDDY	COMPEYSON	EXPECTATIONS	ORLICK
CLARA	HAND	HAVISHAM	HERBERT	ESTELLA
JAGGERS	DRUMMLE	FREE SPACE	PROVIS	AVENGER
FIRE	JOE	STARTOP	GRAVY	MOLLY
BARGEMEN	WEMMICK	MAGWITCH	WOPSLE	PIP

Great Expectations

BIRTHDAY	PORTER	PUMBLECHOOK	POSITION	BLACKSMITH
PIE	MRS JOE	TRABB	BRAG	DICKENS
TUTOR	GREAT	FREE SPACE	GARGERY	JOLLY
LONDON	PIP	WOPSLE	MAGWITCH	WEMMICK
BARGEMEN	MOLLY	GRAVY	STARTOP	JOE

Great Expectations

GRAVEYARD	GREAT	ESTELLA	COMPEYSON	BIDDY
LONDON	PIP	HERBERT	WOPSLE	WEMMICK
PORTER	PUMBLECHOOK	FREE SPACE	JOE	DRUMMLE
CLARA	MRS JOE	BARGEMEN	DICKENS	POSITION
GARGERY	EXPECTATIONS	CLOTHES	BLACKSMITH	BRAG

Great Expectations

STARTOP	HAND	TRABB	MAGWITCH	JOLLY
GRAVY	AGED P	TUTOR	PIE	HAVISHAM
ORLICK	JAGGERS	FREE SPACE	FIRE	AVENGER
MOLLY	BRAG	BLACKSMITH	CLOTHES	EXPECTATIONS
GARGERY	POSITION	DICKENS	BARGEMEN	MRS JOE

Great Expectations

JOE	MAGWITCH	BIDDY	DICKENS	CLOTHES
PIE	AGED P	PUMBLECHOOK	MRS JOE	HERBERT
GREAT	WEMMICK	FREE SPACE	GRAVY	CLARA
PIP	ESTELLA	JAGGERS	POSITION	EXPECTATIONS
COMPEYSON	FIRE	BARGEMEN	STARTOP	AVENGER

Great Expectations

HAVISHAM	GARGERY	PORTER	ORLICK	PROVIS
MOLLY	WOPSLE	TUTOR	BIRTHDAY	JOLLY
DRUMMLE	TRABB	FREE SPACE	GRAVEYARD	BLACKSMITH
LONDON	AVENGER	STARTOP	BARGEMEN	FIRE
COMPEYSON	EXPECTATIONS	POSITION	JAGGERS	ESTELLA

Great Expectations

EXPECTATIONS	MRS JOE	POSITION	CLARA	FIRE
BRAG	WEMMICK	ESTELLA	MOLLY	WOPSLE
PIP	HERBERT	FREE SPACE	BIDDY	BIRTHDAY
JOE	GREAT	PIE	HAND	BARGEMEN
COMPEYSON	BLACKSMITH	CLOTHES	PORTER	GRAVEYARD

Great Expectations

MAGWITCH	PUMBLECHOOK	DICKENS	JAGGERS	PROVIS
HAVISHAM	ORLICK	GARGERY	GRAVY	TUTOR
JOLLY	STARTOP	FREE SPACE	AGED P	TRABB
AVENGER	GRAVEYARD	PORTER	CLOTHES	BLACKSMITH
COMPEYSON	BARGEMEN	HAND	PIE	GREAT

Great Expectations

BIDDY	EXPECTATIONS	BRAG	WEMMICK	CLOTHES
CLARA	POSITION	BLACKSMITH	TUTOR	BARGEMEN
ORLICK	HAND	FREE SPACE	GREAT	PIE
FIRE	HAVISHAM	JAGGERS	AGED P	PORTER
DICKENS	JOE	ESTELLA	PROVIS	LONDON

Great Expectations

COMPEYSON	HERBERT	JOLLY	MRS JOE	AVENGER
MOLLY	GARGERY	PUMBLECHOOK	TRABB	MAGWITCH
GRAVY	STARTOP	FREE SPACE	BIRTHDAY	GRAVEYARD
PIP	LONDON	PROVIS	ESTELLA	JOE
DICKENS	PORTER	AGED P	JAGGERS	HAVISHAM

Great Expectations

BIRTHDAY	AGED P	BIDDY	BRAG	PROVIS
JAGGERS	JOLLY	LONDON	POSITION	WOPSLE
CLARA	PUMBLECHOOK	FREE SPACE	GRAVEYARD	PIP
MOLLY	PIE	GRAVY	BLACKSMITH	DICKENS
DRUMMLE	MAGWITCH	ORLICK	GARGERY	TUTOR

Great Expectations

CLOTHES	JOE	BARGEMEN	GREAT	HERBERT
AVENGER	WEMMICK	PORTER	FIRE	HAVISHAM
HAND	COMPEYSON	FREE SPACE	ESTELLA	EXPECTATIONS
STARTOP	TUTOR	GARGERY	ORLICK	MAGWITCH
DRUMMLE	DICKENS	BLACKSMITH	GRAVY	PIE

Great Expectations

AGED P	EXPECTATIONS	JAGGERS	WEMMICK	JOE
TRABB	BARGEMEN	CLARA	JOLLY	MRS JOE
COMPEYSON	FIRE	FREE SPACE	TUTOR	HAVISHAM
ORLICK	GREAT	PROVIS	GRAVEYARD	DRUMMLE
CLOTHES	MAGWITCH	PIP	STARTOP	PIE

Great Expectations

DICKENS	PORTER	HAND	POSITION	PUMBLECHOOK
AVENGER	WOPSLE	LONDON	GARGERY	ESTELLA
GRAVY	BIRTHDAY	FREE SPACE	BIDDY	MOLLY
HERBERT	PIE	STARTOP	PIP	MAGWITCH
CLOTHES	DRUMMLE	GRAVEYARD	PROVIS	GREAT

Great Expectations

STARTOP	JOE	BRAG	LONDON	GARGERY
JAGGERS	JOLLY	DRUMMLE	EXPECTATIONS	PORTER
HAVISHAM	ESTELLA	FREE SPACE	GREAT	AGED P
WEMMICK	COMPEYSON	GRAVEYARD	WOPSLE	BARGEMEN
DICKENS	MAGWITCH	PIP	TUTOR	MOLLY

Great Expectations

PROVIS	CLARA	MRS JOE	PUMBLECHOOK	HAND
BLACKSMITH	FIRE	POSITION	CLOTHES	BIDDY
AVENGER	ORLICK	FREE SPACE	HERBERT	BIRTHDAY
PIE	MOLLY	TUTOR	PIP	MAGWITCH
DICKENS	BARGEMEN	WOPSLE	GRAVEYARD	COMPEYSON

Great Expectations Vocabulary Word List

No.	Word	Clue/Definition
1.	ABEYANCE	Condition of being temporarily set aside
2.	ABJECT	Contemptible; miserable; wretched
3.	ACQUIESCED	Consented without argument
4.	AGUE	Fever & chills
5.	ALIENATED	Turned away; pushed away
6.	ALLUDED	Suggested indirectly
7.	APPARITION	Ghost
8.	APPROBATION	Approval
9.	ASSIDUITY	Constant personal attention
10.	ASUNDER	Apart from each other
11.	AUGMENTED	Added to
12.	AUGUR	Predict
13.	AUSPICIOUS	Marked by success; grand
14.	AVARICIOUS	Stingy; wanting wealth for oneself
15.	BENEVOLENT	Good
16.	BLITHE	Carefree & lighthearted
17.	CAPRICIOUS	Whimsical
18.	CONNUBIAL	Relating to marriage
19.	CONSIGNED	Entrusted; gave over to the care of another
20.	CONSORTED	Associated
21.	CONSTERNATION	State of paralyzing dismay
22.	CONTIGUOUS	Neighboring; adjacent
23.	CORROBORATED	Supported by other evidence
24.	COUNTENANCES	Faces
25.	DEPOSE	Make a statement of facts
26.	DEPRECIATION	Belittling
27.	DETRIMENTAL	Damaging
28.	DISCONSOLATELY	Gloomily
29.	ELICITING	Bringing out; drawing forth
30.	EPISTLE	Letter
31.	EXCREATING	Cursing
32.	EXECRATED	Denounced
33.	EXHORTED	Urged; advised
34.	EXONERATED	Freed from blame
35.	EXPATRIATED	Removed from residence in one's native land
36.	EXTRICATE	Release from an entanglement
37.	FAIN	Pleased; willing; obliged
38.	FELICITOUS	Lucky
39.	FIDELITY	Faithfulness; loyalty
40.	FORTUITOUSLY	By accident or chance
41.	FUTILE	Having no useful result
42.	IGNOMINIOUSLY	Shamefully; humiliatingly
43.	IMPERIOUSLY	Domineeringly; overbearingly
44.	IMPETUOSITY	Forcefully; passionately
45.	IMPIOUSLY	Lacking reverence, respect or dutifulness
46.	INCONGRUITY	At odds; not matching
47.	INDELIBLE	Permanent
48.	INSOLENT	Arrogant; insulting
49.	INSOLENTLY	Insultingly; rudely
50.	INTIMATION	Hint
51.	INTRICACIES	Complexities
52.	IRRESOLUTE	Undecided
53.	LATENT	Present but not active; hidden

Great Expectations Vocabulary Word List

No.	Word	Clue/Definition
54.	LOITERED	Dawdled; proceeded slowly or with many stops
55.	LUCID	Easily understood
56.	MAGNANIMOUS	Generous in forgiving; noble
57.	MALIGNANT	Disposed towards evil
58.	MOROSE	Melancholy; gloomy
59.	OBDURATE	Hard-hearted; not giving in to persuasion
60.	OBSEQUIOUS	Full of or showing servile compliance
61.	OBSTINATELY	Stubbornly
62.	ODIOUS	Arousing strong dislike
63.	OMNIPOTENT	All-powerful
64.	PERNICIOUS	Destructive; deadly
65.	PERUSED	Looked over with care
66.	PERVADE	Be present throughout
67.	PLAITED	Braided
68.	PRESENTIMENT	Sense that something is about to happen
69.	PREVAILING	Most common; widespread
70.	PROPENSITIES	Tendencies
71.	RAVENOUSLY	Hungrily
72.	RECONNOITRE	Make a preliminary investigation
73.	REFECTORIES	Rooms where meals are served
74.	REPUDIATE	Totally reject
75.	RETICENT	Reserved
76.	SAGACIOUSLY	Intelligently; wisely
77.	SUPERCILIOUSLY	Showing haughty disdain
78.	SYNOPSIS	Summary
79.	TENURE	Period during which something is held
80.	TITHE	One tenth
81.	TRENCHANT	Distinct; forceful, effective & vigorous
82.	TREPIDATION	State of dread or alarm
83.	TRUCULENT	Having a tendency to fight; fierce
84.	UNSCRUPULOUS	Without a conscience or a moral code

Great Expectations Vocabulary Fill In The Blank 1

_____ 1. Arrogant; insulting

_____ 2. Supported by other evidence

_____ 3. Forcefully; passionately

_____ 4. Faithfulness; loyalty

_____ 5. Relating to marriage

_____ 6. Approval

_____ 7. By accident or chance

_____ 8. Damaging

_____ 9. Insultingly; rudely

_____ 10. Distinct; forceful, effective & vigorous

_____ 11. Contemptible; miserable; wretched

_____ 12. Complexities

_____ 13. Gloomily

_____ 14. Condition of being temporarily set aside

_____ 15. Hint

_____ 16. Domineeringly; overbearingly

_____ 17. Showing haughty disdain

_____ 18. Belittling

_____ 19. Most common; widespread

_____ 20. Permanent

Great Expectations Vocabulary Fill In The Blank 1 Answer Key

INSOLENT	1. Arrogant; insulting
CORROBORATED	2. Supported by other evidence
IMPETUOSITY	3. Forcefully; passionately
FIDELITY	4. Faithfulness; loyalty
CONNUBIAL	5. Relating to marriage
APPROBATION	6. Approval
FORTUITOUSLY	7. By accident or chance
DETRIMENTAL	8. Damaging
INSOLENTLY	9. Insultingly; rudely
TRENCHANT	10. Distinct; forceful, effective & vigorous
ABJECT	11. Contemptible; miserable; wretched
INTRICACIES	12. Complexities
DISCONSOLATELY	13. Gloomily
ABEYANCE	14. Condition of being temporarily set aside
INTIMATION	15. Hint
IMPERIOUSLY	16. Domineeringly; overbearingly
SUPERCILIOUSLY	17. Showing haughty disdain
DEPRECIATION	18. Belittling
PREVAILING	19. Most common; widespread
INDELIBLE	20. Permanent

Great Expectations Vocabulary Fill In The Blank 2

_____ 1. Reserved

_____ 2. Lucky

_____ 3. Apart from each other

_____ 4. Looked over with care

_____ 5. Make a preliminary investigation

_____ 6. Having no useful result

_____ 7. Relating to marriage

_____ 8. Removed from residence in one's native land

_____ 9. Tendencies

_____ 10. Complexities

_____ 11. Predict

_____ 12. Approval

_____ 13. Easily understood

_____ 14. Fever & chills

_____ 15. Most common; widespread

_____ 16. Whimsical

_____ 17. At odds; not matching

_____ 18. Faithfulness; loyalty

_____ 19. Undecided

_____ 20. Intelligently; wisely

Great Expectations Vocabulary Fill In The Blank 2 Answer Key

RETICENT	1.	Reserved
FELICITOUS	2.	Lucky
ASUNDER	3.	Apart from each other
PERUSED	4.	Looked over with care
RECONNOITRE	5.	Make a preliminary investigation
FUTILE	6.	Having no useful result
CONNUBIAL	7.	Relating to marriage
EXPATRIATED	8.	Removed from residence in one's native land
PROPENSITIES	9.	Tendencies
INTRICACIES	10.	Complexities
AUGUR	11.	Predict
APPROBATION	12.	Approval
LUCID	13.	Easily understood
AGUE	14.	Fever & chills
PREVAILING	15.	Most common; widespread
CAPRICIOUS	16.	Whimsical
INCONGRUITY	17.	At odds; not matching
FIDELITY	18.	Faithfulness; loyalty
IRRESOLUTE	19.	Undecided
SAGACIOUSLY	20.	Intelligently; wisely

Great Expectations Vocabulary Fill In The Blank 3

1. Letter
2. Fever & chills
3. Damaging
4. Pleased; willing; obliged
5. Faces
6. Having a tendency to fight; fierce
7. Most common; widespread
8. Forcefully; passionately
9. Good
10. Domineeringly; overbearingly
11. Showing haughty disdain
12. Urged; advised
13. State of paralyzing dismay
14. Be present throughout
15. One tenth
16. Entrusted; gave over to the care of another
17. Present but not active; hidden
18. Melancholy; gloomy
19. Added to
20. Dawdled; proceeded slowly or with many stops

Great Expectations Vocabulary Fill in The Blank 3 Answer Key

EPISTLE	1. Letter
AGUE	2. Fever & chills
DETRIMENTAL	3. Damaging
FAIN	4. Pleased; willing; obliged
COUNTENANCES	5. Faces
TRUCULENT	6. Having a tendency to fight; fierce
PREVAILING	7. Most common; widespread
IMPETUOSITY	8. Forcefully; passionately
BENEVOLENT	9. Good
IMPERIOUSLY	10. Domineeringly; overbearingly
SUPERCILIOUSLY	11. Showing haughty disdain
EXHORTED	12. Urged; advised
CONSTERNATION	13. State of paralyzing dismay
PERVADE	14. Be present throughout
TITHE	15. One tenth
CONSIGNED	16. Entrusted; gave over to the care of another
LATENT	17. Present but not active; hidden
MOROSE	18. Melancholy; gloomy
AUGMENTED	19. Added to
LOITERED	20. Dawdled; proceeded slowly or with many stops

Great Expectations Vocabulary Fill In The Blank 4

_____ 1. Freed from blame

_____ 2. Entrusted; gave over to the care of another

_____ 3. Ghost

_____ 4. Braided

_____ 5. State of paralyzing dismay

_____ 6. Constant personal attention

_____ 7. Shamefully; humiliatingly

_____ 8. Pleased; willing; obliged

_____ 9. Sense that something is about to happen

_____ 10. Without a conscience or a moral code

_____ 11. Stubbornly

_____ 12. Urged; advised

_____ 13. Hint

_____ 14. Stingy; wanting wealth for oneself

_____ 15. Be present throughout

_____ 16. Suggested indirectly

_____ 17. Bringing out; drawing forth

_____ 18. Full of or showing servile compliance

_____ 19. Release from an entanglement

_____ 20. Intelligently; wisely

Great Expectations Vocabulary Fill In The Blank 4 Answer Key

EXONERATED	1. Freed from blame
CONSIGNED	2. Entrusted; gave over to the care of another
APPARITION	3. Ghost
PLAITED	4. Braided
CONSTERNATION	5. State of paralyzing dismay
ASSIDUITY	6. Constant personal attention
IGNOMINIOUSLY	7. Shamefully; humiliatingly
FAIN	8. Pleased; willing; obliged
PRESENTIMENT	9. Sense that something is about to happen
UNSCRUPULOUS	10. Without a conscience or a moral code
OBSTINATELY	11. Stubbornly
EXHORTED	12. Urged; advised
INTIMATION	13. Hint
AVARICIOUS	14. Stingy; wanting wealth for oneself
PERVADE	15. Be present throughout
ALLUDED	16. Suggested indirectly
ELICITING	17. Bringing out; drawing forth
OBSEQUIOUS	18. Full of or showing servile compliance
EXTRICATE	19. Release from an entanglement
SAGACIOUSLY	20. Intelligently; wisely

Great Expectations Vocabulary Matching 1

___ 1. CONSIGNED   A. At odds; not matching
___ 2. COUNTENANCES   B. Constant personal attention
___ 3. OBSTINATELY   C. Predict
___ 4. DETRIMENTAL   D. Belittling
___ 5. ASUNDER   E. Urged; advised
___ 6. ABJECT   F. Melancholy; gloomy
___ 7. INSOLENT   G. Looked over with care
___ 8. SAGACIOUSLY   H. Arrogant; insulting
___ 9. AUSPICIOUS   I. Make a preliminary investigation
___ 10. INTIMATION   J. Carefree & lighthearted
___ 11. DISCONSOLATELY   K. State of paralyzing dismay
___ 12. DEPRECIATION   L. Removed from residence in one's native land
___ 13. CONNUBIAL   M. Stubbornly
___ 14. EXPATRIATED   N. Relating to marriage
___ 15. PERUSED   O. Damaging
___ 16. RECONNOITRE   P. Apart from each other
___ 17. AUGUR   Q. Marked by success; grand
___ 18. INCONGRUITY   R. Be present throughout
___ 19. BLITHE   S. Contemptible; miserable; wretched
___ 20. PERVADE   T. Intelligently; wisely
___ 21. CONSTERNATION   U. Entrusted; gave over to the care of another
___ 22. EXHORTED   V. Hint
___ 23. ELICITING   W. Bringing out; drawing forth
___ 24. MOROSE   X. Gloomily
___ 25. ASSIDUITY   Y. Faces

Great Expectations Vocabulary Matching 1 Answer Key

U - 1. CONSIGNED	A.	At odds; not matching
Y - 2. COUNTENANCES	B.	Constant personal attention
M - 3. OBSTINATELY	C.	Predict
O - 4. DETRIMENTAL	D.	Belittling
P - 5. ASUNDER	E.	Urged; advised
S - 6. ABJECT	F.	Melancholy; gloomy
H - 7. INSOLENT	G.	Looked over with care
T - 8. SAGACIOUSLY	H.	Arrogant; insulting
Q - 9. AUSPICIOUS	I.	Make a preliminary investigation
V - 10. INTIMATION	J.	Carefree & lighthearted
X - 11. DISCONSOLATELY	K.	State of paralyzing dismay
D - 12. DEPRECIATION	L.	Removed from residence in one's native land
N - 13. CONNUBIAL	M.	Stubbornly
L - 14. EXPATRIATED	N.	Relating to marriage
G - 15. PERUSED	O.	Damaging
I - 16. RECONNOITRE	P.	Apart from each other
C - 17. AUGUR	Q.	Marked by success; grand
A - 18. INCONGRUITY	R.	Be present throughout
J - 19. BLITHE	S.	Contemptible; miserable; wretched
R - 20. PERVADE	T.	Intelligently; wisely
K - 21. CONSTERNATION	U.	Entrusted; gave over to the care of another
E - 22. EXHORTED	V.	Hint
W - 23. ELICITING	W.	Bringing out; drawing forth
F - 24. MOROSE	X.	Gloomily
B - 25. ASSIDUITY	Y.	Faces

Great Expectations Vocabulary Matching 2

___ 1. OBSTINATELY   A. Lucky
___ 2. FAIN   B. Destructive; deadly
___ 3. BENEVOLENT   C. Constant personal attention
___ 4. INSOLENT   D. Stingy; wanting wealth for oneself
___ 5. EXHORTED   E. Having no useful result
___ 6. IMPETUOSITY   F. Arousing strong dislike
___ 7. LUCID   G. One tenth
___ 8. AUSPICIOUS   H. Ghost
___ 9. SYNOPSIS   I. Faithfulness; loyalty
___ 10. UNSCRUPULOUS   J. Approval
___ 11. ODIOUS   K. Arrogant; insulting
___ 12. TITHE   L. Good
___ 13. FELICITOUS   M. Looked over with care
___ 14. FUTILE   N. Stubbornly
___ 15. APPROBATION   O. Summary
___ 16. PERUSED   P. Pleased; willing; obliged
___ 17. APPARITION   Q. Easily understood
___ 18. FIDELITY   R. Added to
___ 19. INTRICACIES   S. Urged; advised
___ 20. PERNICIOUS   T. Without a conscience or a moral code
___ 21. AVARICIOUS   U. Forcefully; passionately
___ 22. AUGMENTED   V. Complexities
___ 23. ASSIDUITY   W. Marked by success; grand
___ 24. CONSTERNATION   X. Lacking reverence, respect or dutifulness
___ 25. IMPIOUSLY   Y. State of paralyzing dismay

Great Expectations Vocabulary Matching 2 Answer Key

N - 1.	OBSTINATELY	A. Lucky
P - 2.	FAIN	B. Destructive; deadly
L - 3.	BENEVOLENT	C. Constant personal attention
K - 4.	INSOLENT	D. Stingy; wanting wealth for oneself
S - 5.	EXHORTED	E. Having no useful result
U - 6.	IMPETUOSITY	F. Arousing strong dislike
Q - 7.	LUCID	G. One tenth
W - 8.	AUSPICIOUS	H. Ghost
O - 9.	SYNOPSIS	I. Faithfulness; loyalty
T - 10.	UNSCRUPULOUS	J. Approval
F - 11.	ODIOUS	K. Arrogant; insulting
G - 12.	TITHE	L. Good
A - 13.	FELICITOUS	M. Looked over with care
E - 14.	FUTILE	N. Stubbornly
J - 15.	APPROBATION	O. Summary
M - 16.	PERUSED	P. Pleased; willing; obliged
H - 17.	APPARITION	Q. Easily understood
I - 18.	FIDELITY	R. Added to
V - 19.	INTRICACIES	S. Urged; advised
B - 20.	PERNICIOUS	T. Without a conscience or a moral code
D - 21.	AVARICIOUS	U. Forcefully; passionately
R - 22.	AUGMENTED	V. Complexities
C - 23.	ASSIDUITY	W. Marked by success; grand
Y - 24.	CONSTERNATION	X. Lacking reverence, respect or dutifulness
X - 25.	IMPIOUSLY	Y. State of paralyzing dismay

Great Expectations Vocabulary Matching 3

___ 1. IMPERIOUSLY   A. Constant personal attention
___ 2. TRUCULENT   B. Denounced
___ 3. DEPOSE   C. Freed from blame
___ 4. REFECTORIES   D. Make a statement of facts
___ 5. EXONERATED   E. Removed from residence in one's native land
___ 6. INSOLENT   F. Intelligently; wisely
___ 7. AUGUR   G. Gloomily
___ 8. SAGACIOUSLY   H. Having a tendency to fight; fierce
___ 9. ABJECT   I. Hungrily
___10. INCONGRUITY   J. Faces
___11. RETICENT   K. Contemptible; miserable; wretched
___12. CAPRICIOUS   L. At odds; not matching
___13. PROPENSITIES   M. Release from an entanglement
___14. ALIENATED   N. Reserved
___15. INSOLENTLY   O. Whimsical
___16. EXPATRIATED   P. Turned away; pushed away
___17. RAVENOUSLY   Q. Tendencies
___18. COUNTENANCES   R. Predict
___19. PERNICIOUS   S. Bringing out; drawing forth
___20. ASSIDUITY   T. Insultingly; rudely
___21. EXTRICATE   U. Rooms where meals are served
___22. DISCONSOLATELY   V. Having no useful result
___23. ELICITING   W. Arrogant; insulting
___24. FUTILE   X. Domineeringly; overbearingly
___25. EXECRATED   Y. Destructive; deadly

Great Expectations Vocabulary Matching 3 Answer Key

X - 1. IMPERIOUSLY	A.	Constant personal attention
H - 2. TRUCULENT	B.	Denounced
D - 3. DEPOSE	C.	Freed from blame
U - 4. REFECTORIES	D.	Make a statement of facts
C - 5. EXONERATED	E.	Removed from residence in one's native land
W - 6. INSOLENT	F.	Intelligently; wisely
R - 7. AUGUR	G.	Gloomily
F - 8. SAGACIOUSLY	H.	Having a tendency to fight; fierce
K - 9. ABJECT	I.	Hungrily
L - 10. INCONGRUITY	J.	Faces
N - 11. RETICENT	K.	Contemptible; miserable; wretched
O - 12. CAPRICIOUS	L.	At odds; not matching
Q - 13. PROPENSITIES	M.	Release from an entanglement
P - 14. ALIENATED	N.	Reserved
T - 15. INSOLENTLY	O.	Whimsical
E - 16. EXPATRIATED	P.	Turned away; pushed away
I - 17. RAVENOUSLY	Q.	Tendencies
J - 18. COUNTENANCES	R.	Predict
Y - 19. PERNICIOUS	S.	Bringing out; drawing forth
A - 20. ASSIDUITY	T.	Insultingly; rudely
M - 21. EXTRICATE	U.	Rooms where meals are served
G - 22. DISCONSOLATELY	V.	Having no useful result
S - 23. ELICITING	W.	Arrogant; insulting
V - 24. FUTILE	X.	Domineeringly; overbearingly
B - 25. EXECRATED	Y.	Destructive; deadly

Great Expectations Vocabulary Matching 4

___ 1. SAGACIOUSLY   A. Hard-hearted; not giving in to persuasion
___ 2. MAGNANIMOUS   B. Full of or showing servile compliance
___ 3. CONSIGNED   C. Gloomily
___ 4. RECONNOITRE   D. Hungrily
___ 5. INSOLENT   E. Lacking reverence, respect or dutifulness
___ 6. COUNTENANCES   F. Predict
___ 7. AUGMENTED   G. Damaging
___ 8. TITHE   H. Faces
___ 9. TRENCHANT   I. One tenth
___10. IMPIOUSLY   J. Good
___11. UNSCRUPULOUS   K. Relating to marriage
___12. OBDURATE   L. Destructive; deadly
___13. DISCONSOLATELY   M. Generous in forgiving; noble
___14. OBSEQUIOUS   N. Arrogant; insulting
___15. PERNICIOUS   O. Added to
___16. RAVENOUSLY   P. Without a conscience or a moral code
___17. INTIMATION   Q. Distinct; forceful, effective & vigorous
___18. TENURE   R. Intelligently; wisely
___19. CONNUBIAL   S. Forcefully; passionately
___20. CAPRICIOUS   T. Hint
___21. INTRICACIES   U. Period during which something is held
___22. IMPETUOSITY   V. Make a preliminary investigation
___23. BENEVOLENT   W. Whimsical
___24. DETRIMENTAL   X. Complexities
___25. AUGUR   Y. Entrusted; gave over to the care of another

Great Expectations Vocabulary Matching 4 Answer Key

R - 1.	SAGACIOUSLY	A. Hard-hearted; not giving in to persuasion
M - 2.	MAGNANIMOUS	B. Full of or showing servile compliance
Y - 3.	CONSIGNED	C. Gloomily
V - 4.	RECONNOITRE	D. Hungrily
N - 5.	INSOLENT	E. Lacking reverence, respect or dutifulness
H - 6.	COUNTENANCES	F. Predict
O - 7.	AUGMENTED	G. Damaging
I - 8.	TITHE	H. Faces
Q - 9.	TRENCHANT	I. One tenth
E - 10.	IMPIOUSLY	J. Good
P - 11.	UNSCRUPULOUS	K. Relating to marriage
A - 12.	OBDURATE	L. Destructive; deadly
C - 13.	DISCONSOLATELY	M. Generous in forgiving; noble
B - 14.	OBSEQUIOUS	N. Arrogant; insulting
L - 15.	PERNICIOUS	O. Added to
D - 16.	RAVENOUSLY	P. Without a conscience or a moral code
T - 17.	INTIMATION	Q. Distinct; forceful, effective & vigorous
U - 18.	TENURE	R. Intelligently; wisely
K - 19.	CONNUBIAL	S. Forcefully; passionately
W - 20.	CAPRICIOUS	T. Hint
X - 21.	INTRICACIES	U. Period during which something is held
S - 22.	IMPETUOSITY	V. Make a preliminary investigation
J - 23.	BENEVOLENT	W. Whimsical
G - 24.	DETRIMENTAL	X. Complexities
F - 25.	AUGUR	Y. Entrusted; gave over to the care of another

Great Expectations Vocabulary Magic Squares 1

Match the definition with the vocabulary word. Put your answers in the magic squares below. When your answers are correct, all columns and rows will add to the same number.

A. PERUSED
B. OBSEQUIOUS
C. OMNIPOTENT
D. INTIMATION
E. INSOLENT
F. EXPATRIATED
G. OBDURATE
H. ALLUDED
I. BENEVOLENT
J. MOROSE
K. BLITHE
L. IMPIOUSLY
M. LOITERED
N. ASUNDER
O. FELICITOUS
P. TREPIDATION

1. Lucky
2. Melancholy; gloomy
3. Suggested indirectly
4. Looked over with care
5. Hint
6. Arrogant; insulting
7. Carefree & lighthearted
8. Apart from each other
9. Removed from residence in one's native land
10. All-powerful
11. Dawdled; proceeded slowly or with many stops
12. Lacking reverence, respect or dutifulness
13. Good
14. State of dread or alarm
15. Full of or showing servile compliance
16. Hard-hearted; not giving in to persuasion

A=	B=	C=	D=
E=	F=	G=	H=
I=	J=	K=	L=
M=	N=	O=	P=

Great Expectations Vocabulary Magic Squares 1 Answer Key

Match the definition with the vocabulary word. Put your answers in the magic squares below. When your answers are correct, all columns and rows will add to the same number.

A. PERUSED
B. OBSEQUIOUS
C. OMNIPOTENT
D. INTIMATION
E. INSOLENT
F. EXPATRIATED
G. OBDURATE
H. ALLUDED
I. BENEVOLENT
J. MOROSE
K. BLITHE
L. IMPIOUSLY
M. LOITERED
N. ASUNDER
O. FELICITOUS
P. TREPIDATION

1. Lucky
2. Melancholy; gloomy
3. Suggested indirectly
4. Looked over with care
5. Hint
6. Arrogant; insulting
7. Carefree & lighthearted
8. Apart from each other
9. Removed from residence in one's native land
10. All-powerful
11. Dawdled; proceeded slowly or with many stops
12. Lacking reverence, respect or dutifulness
13. Good
14. State of dread or alarm
15. Full of or showing servile compliance
16. Hard-hearted; not giving in to persuasion

A=4	B=15	C=10	D=5
E=6	F=9	G=16	H=3
I=13	J=2	K=7	L=12
M=11	N=8	O=1	P=14

Great Expectations Vocabulary Magic Squares 2

Match the definition with the vocabulary word. Put your answers in the magic squares below. When your answers are correct, all columns and rows will add to the same number.

A. RETICENT
B. PRESENTIMENT
C. ASUNDER
D. AUGMENTED
E. CORROBORATED
F. ABEYANCE
G. REFECTORIES
H. TENURE
I. PERNICIOUS
J. TRENCHANT
K. TRUCULENT
L. OBDURATE
M. MALIGNANT
N. CONSORTED
O. CONTIGUOUS
P. BLITHE

1. Neighboring; adjacent
2. Added to
3. Distinct; forceful, effective & vigorous
4. Supported by other evidence
5. Destructive; deadly
6. Condition of being temporarily set aside
7. Carefree & lighthearted
8. Apart from each other
9. Period during which something is held
10. Having a tendency to fight; fierce
11. Reserved
12. Associated
13. Sense that something is about to happen
14. Disposed towards evil
15. Rooms where meals are served
16. Hard-hearted; not giving in to persuasion

A=	B=	C=	D=
E=	F=	G=	H=
I=	J=	K=	L=
M=	N=	O=	P=

Great Expectations Vocabulary Magic Squares 2 Answer Key

Match the definition with the vocabulary word. Put your answers in the magic squares below. When your answers are correct, all columns and rows will add to the same number.

A. RETICENT
B. PRESENTIMENT
C. ASUNDER
D. AUGMENTED
E. CORROBORATED
F. ABEYANCE
G. REFECTORIES
H. TENURE
I. PERNICIOUS
J. TRENCHANT
K. TRUCULENT
L. OBDURATE
M. MALIGNANT
N. CONSORTED
O. CONTIGUOUS
P. BLITHE

1. Neighboring; adjacent
2. Added to
3. Distinct; forceful, effective & vigorous
4. Supported by other evidence
5. Destructive; deadly
6. Condition of being temporarily set aside
7. Carefree & lighthearted
8. Apart from each other
9. Period during which something is held
10. Having a tendency to fight; fierce
11. Reserved
12. Associated
13. Sense that something is about to happen
14. Disposed towards evil
15. Rooms where meals are served
16. Hard-hearted; not giving in to persuasion

A=11	B=13	C=8	D=2
E=4	F=6	G=15	H=9
I=5	J=3	K=10	L=16
M=14	N=12	O=1	P=7

Great Expectations Vocabulary Magic Squares 3

Match the definition with the vocabulary word. Put your answers in the magic squares below. When your answers are correct, all columns and rows will add to the same number.

A. ACQUIESCED
B. PREVAILING
C. OBSEQUIOUS
D. INSOLENTLY
E. DEPRECIATION
F. SUPERCILIOUSLY
G. MOROSE
H. ALIENATED
I. INTRICACIES
J. EXTRICATE
K. ASUNDER
L. INTIMATION
M. APPROBATION
N. REFECTORIES
O. FIDELITY
P. FAIN

1. Full of or showing servile compliance
2. Release from an entanglement
3. Showing haughty disdain
4. Faithfulness; loyalty
5. Pleased; willing; obliged
6. Belittling
7. Complexities
8. Insultingly; rudely
9. Approval
10. Turned away; pushed away
11. Hint
12. Consented without argument
13. Most common; widespread
14. Apart from each other
15. Melancholy; gloomy
16. Rooms where meals are served

A=	B=	C=	D=
E=	F=	G=	H=
I=	J=	K=	L=
M=	N=	O=	P=

Great Expectations Vocabulary Magic Squares 3 Answer Key

Match the definition with the vocabulary word. Put your answers in the magic squares below. When your answers are correct, all columns and rows will add to the same number.

A. ACQUIESCED
B. PREVAILING
C. OBSEQUIOUS
D. INSOLENTLY
E. DEPRECIATION
F. SUPERCILIOUSLY
G. MOROSE
H. ALIENATED
I. INTRICACIES
J. EXTRICATE
K. ASUNDER
L. INTIMATION
M. APPROBATION
N. REFECTORIES
O. FIDELITY
P. FAIN

1. Full of or showing servile compliance
2. Release from an entanglement
3. Showing haughty disdain
4. Faithfulness; loyalty
5. Pleased; willing; obliged
6. Belittling
7. Complexities
8. Insultingly; rudely
9. Approval
10. Turned away; pushed away
11. Hint
12. Consented without argument
13. Most common; widespread
14. Apart from each other
15. Melancholy; gloomy
16. Rooms where meals are served

A=12	B=13	C=1	D=8
E=6	F=3	G=15	H=10
I=7	J=2	K=14	L=11
M=9	N=16	O=4	P=5

Great Expectations Vocabulary Magic Squares 4

Match the definition with the vocabulary word. Put your answers in the magic squares below. When your answers are correct, all columns and rows will add to the same number.

A. EXHORTED
B. ODIOUS
C. INDELIBLE
D. EXECRATED
E. FAIN
F. CONSIGNED
G. OBSEQUIOUS
H. PERVADE
I. INTRICACIES
J. CORROBORATED
K. TRUCULENT
L. DISCONSOLATELY
M. LUCID
N. PROPENSITIES
O. EXCREATING
P. AUGMENTED

1. Urged; advised
2. Tendencies
3. Supported by other evidence
4. Pleased; willing; obliged
5. Full of or showing servile compliance
6. Gloomily
7. Added to
8. Permanent
9. Cursing
10. Denounced
11. Be present throughout
12. Having a tendency to fight; fierce
13. Complexities
14. Entrusted; gave over to the care of another
15. Arousing strong dislike
16. Easily understood

A=	B=	C=	D=
E=	F=	G=	H=
I=	J=	K=	L=
M=	N=	O=	P=

Great Expectations Vocabulary Magic Squares 4 Answer Key

Match the definition with the vocabulary word. Put your answers in the magic squares below. When your answers are correct, all columns and rows will add to the same number.

A. EXHORTED
B. ODIOUS
C. INDELIBLE
D. EXECRATED
E. FAIN
F. CONSIGNED
G. OBSEQUIOUS
H. PERVADE
I. INTRICACIES
J. CORROBORATED
K. TRUCULENT
L. DISCONSOLATELY
M. LUCID
N. PROPENSITIES
O. EXCREATING
P. AUGMENTED

1. Urged; advised
2. Tendencies
3. Supported by other evidence
4. Pleased; willing; obliged
5. Full of or showing servile compliance
6. Gloomily
7. Added to
8. Permanent
9. Cursing
10. Denounced
11. Be present throughout
12. Having a tendency to fight; fierce
13. Complexities
14. Entrusted; gave over to the care of another
15. Arousing strong dislike
16. Easily understood

A=1	B=15	C=8	D=10
E=4	F=14	G=5	H=11
I=13	J=3	K=12	L=6
M=16	N=2	O=9	P=7

Great Expectations Vocabulary Word Search 1

```
E L T S I P E K R R B R A M G P Z V Y V
S V S Y P E R U S E D S B C K L Z A K V
O A U M N R A E H Y F B J L Z A B C K W
R P O N T N G J S B Q E E N I I M Q Y D
O P I Q N I U T N E L U C U R T R U L P
M A U N S C E D L C N O T T Z E H I E D
F R Q W S I Y I X D U T R Y O D Z E T R
F I E P R O T K C N G E I P C R M S A G
Z T S Y S U L O T O C N M M F Z I C L V
X I B W F S N E I O R U P R E L C E O R
D O O L M S N N N R T R I J L N Q D S S
R N D Z O A D N D T R E O P Q G T R N S
E J N R N I O E G L L E U B N L U S O B
P V T C Q I T T P S H Y S I O G U G C P
U E E Q T R V E T O T R L O U R H C S Z
D S K R O N Y N R R S I Y A L S A W I K
I C E H D J E V C E A E T F A U H T D D
A H X R I L R D B V D T D H T S T P E N
T E P N O S K N E R A U G M E N T E D D
E C X S U C G R X T N A H C N E R T Z V
S L N S S B P T R E P I D A T I O N Q J
G I M P E R I O U S L Y O B D U R A T E
```

Added to (9)
Arousing strong dislike (6)
Arrogant; insulting (8)
Associated (9)
Braided (7)
Carefree & lighthearted (6)
Consented without argument (10)
Contemptible; miserable; wretched (6)
Dawdled; proceeded slowly or with many stops (8)
Destructive; deadly (10)
Distinct; forceful, effective & vigorous (9)
Domineeringly; overbearingly (11)
Easily understood (5)
Faces (12)
Fever & chills (4)
Full of or showing servile compliance (10)
Ghost (10)
Gloomily (14)
Hard-hearted; not giving in to persuasion (8)
Having a tendency to fight; fierce (9)
Having no useful result (6)
Insultingly; rudely (10)
Lacking reverence, respect or dutifulness (9)

Letter (7)
Looked over with care (7)
Make a preliminary investigation (11)
Make a statement of facts (6)
Melancholy; gloomy (6)
Most common; widespread (10)
One tenth (5)
Period during which something is held (6)
Pleased; willing; obliged (4)
Predict (5)
Present but not active; hidden (6)
Rooms where meals are served (11)
Sense that something is about to happen (12)
State of dread or alarm (11)
Supported by other evidence (12)
Totally reject (9)
Undecided (10)
Urged; advised (8)

Great Expectations Vocabulary Word Search 1 Answer Key

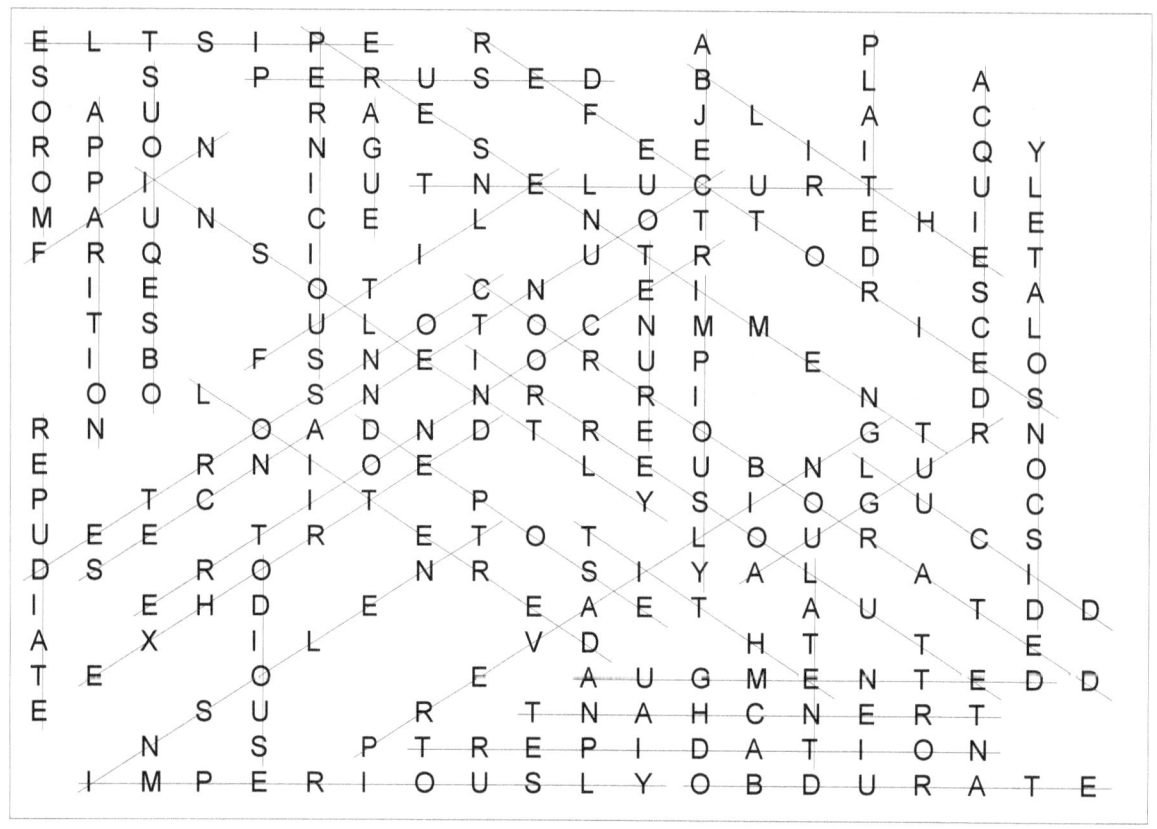

Added to (9)
Arousing strong dislike (6)
Arrogant; insulting (8)
Associated (9)
Braided (7)
Carefree & lighthearted (6)
Consented without argument (10)
Contemptible; miserable; wretched (6)
Dawdled; proceeded slowly or with many stops (8)
Destructive; deadly (10)
Distinct; forceful, effective & vigorous (9)
Domineeringly; overbearingly (11)
Easily understood (5)
Faces (12)
Fever & chills (4)
Full of or showing servile compliance (10)
Ghost (10)
Gloomily (14)
Hard-hearted; not giving in to persuasion (8)
Having a tendency to fight; fierce (9)
Having no useful result (6)
Insultingly; rudely (10)
Lacking reverence, respect or dutifulness (9)

Letter (7)
Looked over with care (7)
Make a preliminary investigation (11)
Make a statement of facts (6)
Melancholy; gloomy (6)
Most common; widespread (10)
One tenth (5)
Period during which something is held (6)
Pleased; willing; obliged (4)
Predict (5)
Present but not active; hidden (6)
Rooms where meals are served (11)
Sense that something is about to happen (12)
State of dread or alarm (11)
Supported by other evidence (12)
Totally reject (9)
Undecided (10)
Urged; advised (8)

Great Expectations Vocabulary Word Search 2

```
A S S I D U I T Y D X T S Y N O P S I S
B L G E L R M W E E E N R P A L D G D H
E M I V L F Q C U D L E E E B U J B Z
Y O R E Q I S Y G U B L P P N R J C J X
A R B K N E C T A L I O I S L C U E I G
N O N S I A Y I B L L S S E A A H S C D
C S D U E J T L T A E N T I S Y I A E T
E E Q N D Q I E X I D I L T U I J T N D
R C Y O E P U D D Y N J E I N N Z D E T
A E L I T K R I W L I G F S D T K E E D
H V T T A S G F O S J T Y N E R B T R S
R T N I R K N Z P U B T S E R I B R U J
T N E R C X O O S O S Q V P L C L O N T
M N L A E E C W D T T P M O W A I H E B
E O O P X G N I L I A V E R P C T X T Q
X I S P E I I T T U O S Z P I I H E Q B
T T N A A F M H R T L U V P X E E S N G
R A I F D R E M B R Y F S S L S S O X T
I M P I O U S L Y O S U O I C I R P A C
C I P E R V A D E F A Y T L Z N U E H X
A T I G N O M I N I O U S L Y Y G D X F
T N A N G I L A M S F Q E T A R U D B O
E I R I M P E T U O S I T Y P Q A P H Q
```

Apart from each other (7)
Arousing strong dislike (6)
Arrogant; insulting (8)
At odds; not matching (11)
Be present throughout (7)
Braided (7)
Bringing out; drawing forth (9)
By accident or chance (12)
Carefree & lighthearted (6)
Complexities (11)
Condition of being temporarily set aside (8)
Consented without argument (10)
Constant personal attention (9)
Contemptible; miserable; wretched (6)
Denounced (9)
Disposed towards evil (9)
Distinct; forceful, effective & vigorous (9)
Easily understood (5)
Faithfulness; loyalty (8)
Fever & chills (4)
Forcefully; passionately (11)
Full of or showing servile compliance (10)
Ghost (10)
Hard-hearted; not giving in to persuasion (8)
Having no useful result (6)

Hint (10)
Insultingly; rudely (10)
Lacking reverence, respect or dutifulness (9)
Letter (7)
Looked over with care (7)
Make a statement of facts (6)
Marked by success; grand (10)
Melancholy; gloomy (6)
Most common; widespread (10)
One tenth (5)
Period during which something is held (6)
Permanent (9)
Pleased; willing; obliged (4)
Predict (5)
Present but not active; hidden (6)
Release from an entanglement (9)
Reserved (8)
Shamefully; humiliatingly (13)
Suggested indirectly (7)
Summary (8)
Tendencies (12)
Turned away; pushed away (9)
Urged; advised (8)
Whimsical (10)

Great Expectations Vocabulary Word Search 2 Answer Key

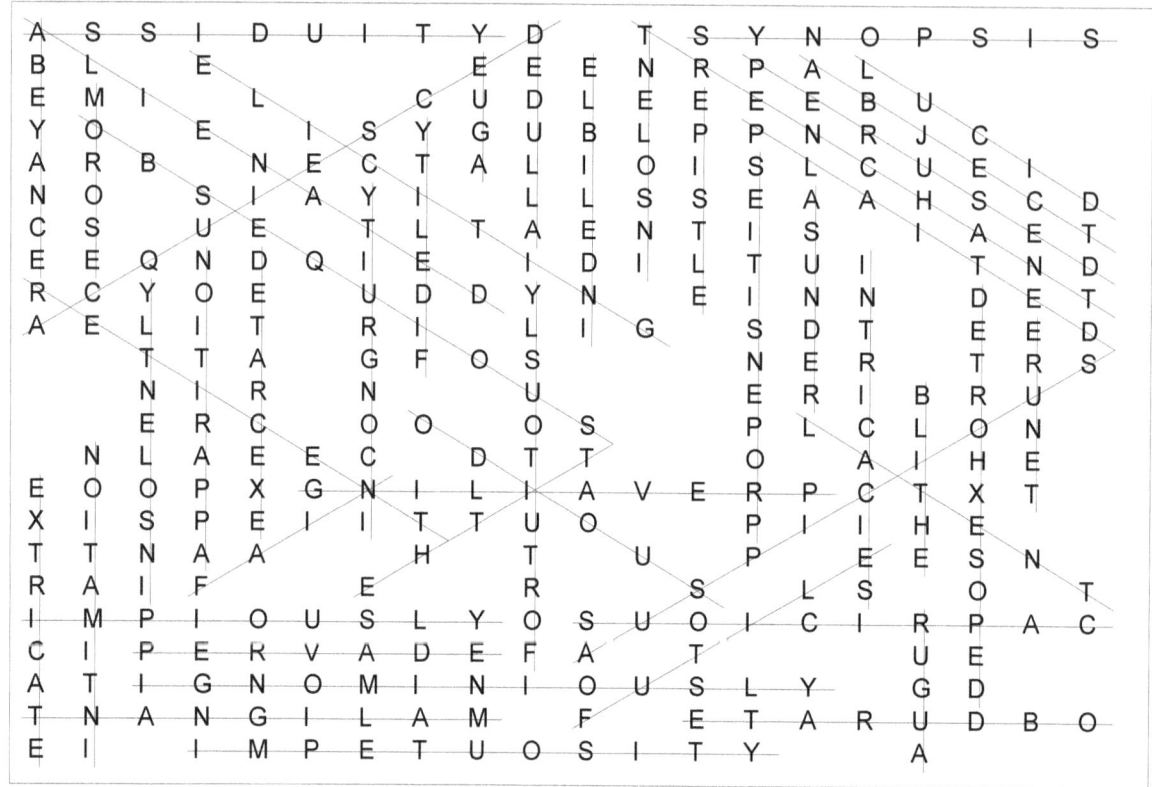

Apart from each other (7)
Arousing strong dislike (6)
Arrogant; insulting (8)
At odds; not matching (11)
Be present throughout (7)
Braided (7)
Bringing out; drawing forth (9)
By accident or chance (12)
Carefree & lighthearted (6)
Complexities (11)
Condition of being temporarily set aside (8)
Consented without argument (10)
Constant personal attention (9)
Contemptible; miserable; wretched (6)
Denounced (9)
Disposed towards evil (9)
Distinct; forceful, effective & vigorous (9)
Easily understood (5)
Faithfulness; loyalty (8)
Fever & chills (4)
Forcefully; passionately (11)
Full of or showing servile compliance (10)
Ghost (10)
Hard-hearted; not giving in to persuasion (8)
Having no useful result (6)

Hint (10)
Insultingly; rudely (10)
Lacking reverence, respect or dutifulness (9)
Letter (7)
Looked over with care (7)
Make a statement of facts (6)
Marked by success; grand (10)
Melancholy; gloomy (6)
Most common; widespread (10)
One tenth (5)
Period during which something is held (6)
Permanent (9)
Pleased; willing; obliged (4)
Predict (5)
Present but not active; hidden (6)
Release from an entanglement (9)
Reserved (8)
Shamefully; humiliatingly (13)
Suggested indirectly (7)
Summary (8)
Tendencies (12)
Turned away; pushed away (9)
Urged; advised (8)
Whimsical (10)

Great Expectations Vocabulary Word Search 3

```
I  M  P  I  O  S  L  Y  T  R  U  C  U  L  E  N  T  R  P
Z  P  Q  H  B  M  I  G  Z  F  P  W  J  R  T  L  I  N  P
D  E  D  Z  S  M  N  N  D  D  N  L  Y  A  A  I  R  A  C
P  R  E  S  E  N  T  I  M  E  N  T  C  S  C  C  R  N  F
R  N  T  U  Q  T  I  L  P  W  Z  I  V  C  Q  I  E  G  N
D  I  A  O  U  R  M  I  Y  O  R  F  F  O  U  T  S  I  R
P  C  R  T  I  E  A  A  Y  T  T  D  A  U  I  I  O  L  B
T  I  O  I  O  P  T  V  X  I  N  E  I  G  E  N  L  A  G
A  O  B  C  U  I  I  E  O  T  E  D  N  I  S  G  U  M  G
U  U  O  I  S  D  O  R  B  H  L  U  T  T  C  P  T  X  A
G  S  R  L  X  A  N  P  S  E  O  L  R  N  E  Y  E  L  B  X
M  P  R  E  M  T  S  M  T  Z  S  L  I  O  D  W  D  E  W  X
E  M  O  F  O  I  D  U  I  F  N  A  C  C  V  E  Y  T  X  R
N  I  C  N  R  O  J  F  N  T  I  U  A  J  T  A  Z  N  D  T
T  C  N  V  O  N  I  R  A  D  Q  G  C  A  N  V  Z  E  Y  V
E  N  H  D  S  D  B  D  T  D  E  U  I  C  G  A  T  T  X  Q
D  A  B  J  E  C  T  D  E  S  U  R  E  P  E  R  V  A  D  E
S  F  V  L  M  L  M  T  L  P  T  M  S  G  O  I  B  L  H  S
N  U  I  G  C  W  I  T  Y  A  O  J  N  S  L  C  C  F  P  N
K  T  A  S  R  A  X  B  P  Q  H  S  N  B  L  I  T  H  E  K
Y  I  X  G  L  R  Q  X  L  F  J  O  E  S  U  O  I  D  O  Y
W  L  D  P  U  Q  E  H  H  E  C  H  W  D  L  U  C  I  D  S
T  E  N  U  R  E  B  I  M  P  E  R  I  O  U  S  L  Y  X  G
```

ABEYANCE	CORROBORATED	INSOLENT	PERNICIOUS
ABJECT	DEPOSE	INTIMATION	PERUSED
ACQUIESCED	ELICITING	INTRICACIES	PERVADE
AGUE	EXPATRIATED	IRRESOLUTE	PLAITED
ALLUDED	EXTRICATE	LATENT	PRESENTIMENT
ASUNDER	FAIN	LUCID	PREVAILING
AUGMENTED	FELICITOUS	MALIGNANT	REPUDIATE
AUGUR	FIDELITY	MOROSE	TENURE
AVARICIOUS	FUTILE	OBSEQUIOUS	TITHE
BLITHE	IMPERIOUSLY	OBSTINATELY	TREPIDATION
CONSORTED	IMPIOUSLY	ODIOUS	TRUCULENT
CONTIGUOUS	INDELIBLE	OMNIPOTENT	

Great Expectations Vocabulary Word Search 3 Answer Key

ABEYANCE	CORROBORATED	INSOLENT	PERNICIOUS
ABJECT	DEPOSE	INTIMATION	PERUSED
ACQUIESCED	ELICITING	INTRICACIES	PERVADE
AGUE	EXPATRIATED	IRRESOLUTE	PLAITED
ALLUDED	EXTRICATE	LATENT	PRESENTIMENT
ASUNDER	FAIN	LUCID	PREVAILING
AUGMENTED	FELICITOUS	MALIGNANT	REPUDIATE
AUGUR	FIDELITY	MOROSE	TENURE
AVARICIOUS	FUTILE	OBSEQUIOUS	TITHE
BLITHE	IMPERIOUSLY	OBSTINATELY	TREPIDATION
CONSORTED	IMPIOUSLY	ODIOUS	TRUCULENT
CONTIGUOUS	INDELIBLE	OMNIPOTENT	

Great Expectations Vocabulary Word Search 4

```
A N N E X E C R A T E D E N G I S N O C
B H O A E F I D E L I T Y S X B A L T N
J N I Y P W N H C N G K N B H K G N X Z
E D T L I P T T F M N A L I E N A T E D
C S A S S I A G U D O D D P S Z C I E X
T H N U T A J R T P M G L E N W I N C T
L L R O L L G G I W I L N F P N O S N F
T A E I E U Q U L T N O O A G O U O A W
E X T R I C A T E Y I M P I O U S L Y H
K K S E Z I K R T T O A N T E L E E C
J E N P N D X I A I U P L I E Y N B V
S X O M P T U D N S S I L R I P R T A Z
B O C I X D I B H O L N O A X G E E V L
A N K S I P W X B U Y T F S I R N T D B
L E H S E F M D T T C I P U U T J A D L
L R S R U G U A D E H M P N E Y E E N C
U A T B D R K G F P P A E D S X S D B T
D T P Y A C G E W M W T G E O U S A L Q
E E K T D J R W G I Z I V R R U F V I V
D D E T A R O B O R R O C E O J X R T B
A U G M E N T E D Z M N P I M Q J E H C
I N C O N G R U I T Y P D D G Z X P E D
A U S P I C I O U S U O I U Q E S B O Y
```

ABEYANCE	CONSIGNED	IMPERIOUSLY	OBSEQUIOUS
ABJECT	CONSTERNATION	IMPETUOSITY	ODIOUS
AGUE	CORROBORATED	IMPIOUSLY	PERUSED
ALIENATED	DEPOSE	INCONGRUITY	PERVADE
ALLUDED	EPISTLE	INSOLENT	PLAITED
APPARITION	EXECRATED	INTIMATION	REFECTORIES
ASSIDUITY	EXONERATED	LATENT	SAGACIOUSLY
ASUNDER	EXTRICATE	LOITERED	TENURE
AUGMENTED	FAIN	LUCID	TITHE
AUGUR	FIDELITY	MALIGNANT	TREPIDATION
AUSPICIOUS	FUTILE	MOROSE	
BLITHE	IGNOMINIOUSLY	OBDURATE	

Great Expectations Vocabulary Word Search 4 Answer Key

ABEYANCE	CONSIGNED	IMPERIOUSLY	OBSEQUIOUS
ABJECT	CONSTERNATION	IMPETUOSITY	ODIOUS
AGUE	CORROBORATED	IMPIOUSLY	PERUSED
ALIENATED	DEPOSE	INCONGRUITY	PERVADE
ALLUDED	EPISTLE	INSOLENT	PLAITED
APPARITION	EXECRATED	INTIMATION	REFECTORIES
ASSIDUITY	EXONERATED	LATENT	SAGACIOUSLY
ASUNDER	EXTRICATE	LOITERED	TENURE
AUGMENTED	FAIN	LUCID	TITHE
AUGUR	FIDELITY	MALIGNANT	TREPIDATION
AUSPICIOUS	FUTILE	MOROSE	
BLITHE	IGNOMINIOUSLY	OBDURATE	

Great Expectations Vocabulary Crossword 1

Across
1. Make a statement of facts
3. Dawdled; proceeded slowly or with many stops
6. Added to
7. Arousing strong dislike
8. Hint
11. Permanent
13. One tenth
16. Pleased; willing; obliged
19. Present but not active; hidden
20. Fever & chills
21. Release from an entanglement
22. Period during which something is held
23. Suggested indirectly
24. Totally reject

Down
1. Damaging
2. Braided
4. Letter
5. Destructive; deadly
7. Hard-hearted; not giving in to persuasion
9. Disposed towards evil
10. Undecided
12. Easily understood
14. Arrogant; insulting
15. Associated
17. Looked over with care
18. Having no useful result
20. Predict

Great Expectations Vocabulary Crossword 1 Answer Key

	1 D	2 E	P	O	S	E			3 L	O	I	T	E	R	4 E	D	
	E		L					5 P						P		
	T	6 A	U	G	M	E	N	T	E	D					I		
	R		I					R		7 O	D	I	O	U	S	
	8 I	N	T	9 I	M	A	10 T	I	O	N		B			T	
	M		E	A			R			11 I	N	D	E	12 L	I	B	L	E
	E		D	L			R			C		U		U			E
	N		13 T	I	T	H	E			I		R		C		
	T		14 I		G		S			O		A		I			15 C
16 F	A	I	N		N		O			U		T		D			O
	L		S		A		L			S		E					N
			O		N		U				17 P			18 F			S
			19 L	A	T	E	N	T			E			U			O
20 A	G	U	E				21 E	X	T	R	I	C	A	T	E		R
U			N				U						I				T
G			22 T	E	N	U	R	E		23 A	L	L	U	D	E	D
U							S						E			D
24 R	E	P	U	D	I	A	T	E		D						

Across
1. Make a statement of facts
3. Dawdled; proceeded slowly or with many stops
6. Added to
7. Arousing strong dislike
8. Hint
11. Permanent
13. One tenth
16. Pleased; willing; obliged
19. Present but not active; hidden
20. Fever & chills
21. Release from an entanglement
22. Period during which something is held
23. Suggested indirectly
24. Totally reject

Down
1. Damaging
2. Braided
4. Letter
5. Destructive; deadly
7. Hard-hearted; not giving in to persuasion
9. Disposed towards evil
10. Undecided
12. Easily understood
14. Arrogant; insulting
15. Associated
17. Looked over with care
18. Having no useful result
20. Predict

Great Expectations Vocabulary Crossword 2

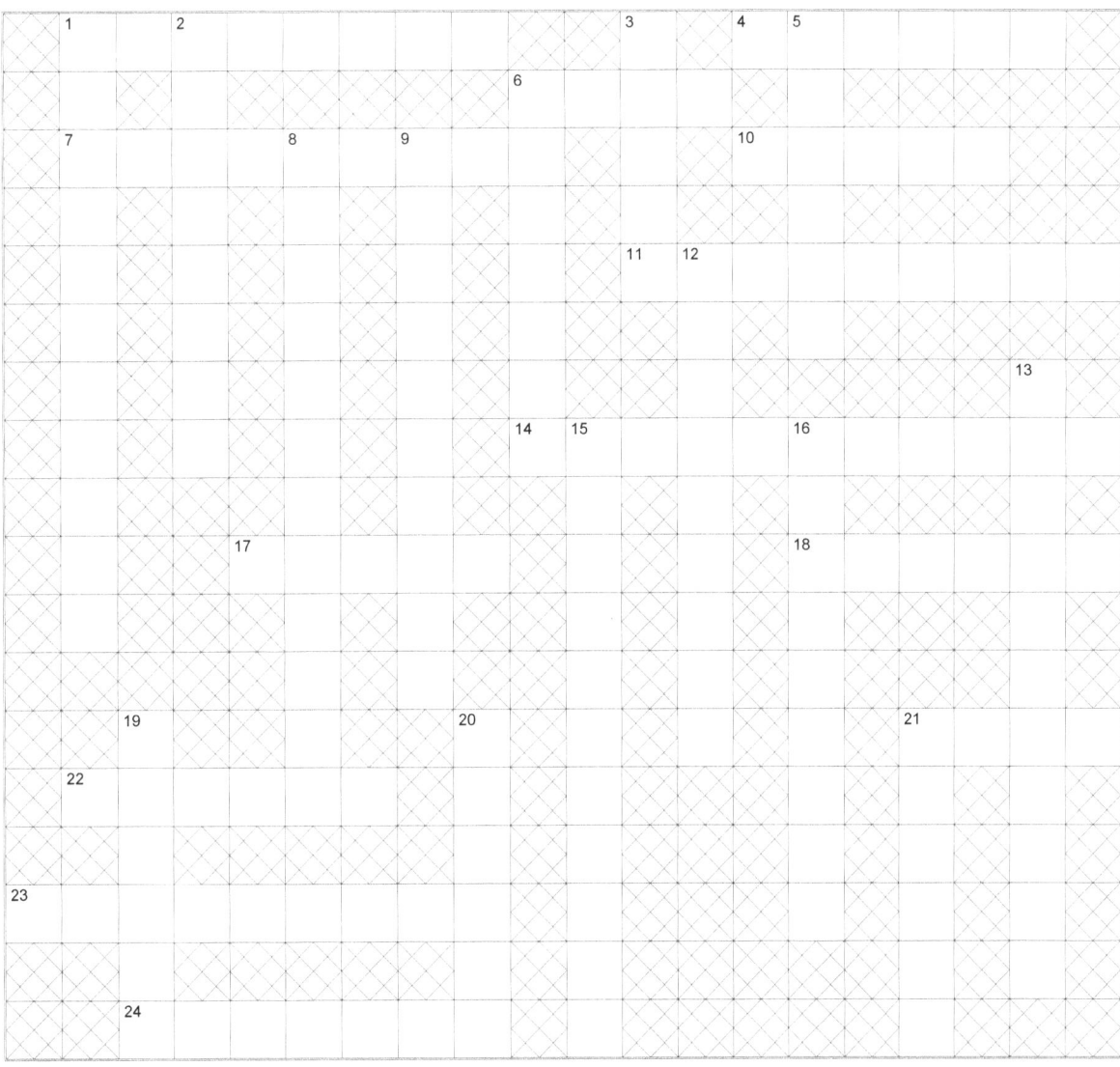

Across
1. Arrogant; insulting
4. Melancholy; gloomy
6. Fever & chills
7. Relating to marriage
10. One tenth
11. Totally reject
14. Damaging
17. Easily understood
18. Present but not active; hidden
21. Pleased; willing; obliged
22. Make a statement of facts
23. Having a tendency to fight; fierce
24. Letter

Down
1. At odds; not matching
2. Summary
3. Predict
5. Arousing strong dislike
6. Suggested indirectly
8. Without a conscience or a moral code
9. Hint
12. Release from an entanglement
13. Generous in forgiving; noble
15. Removed from residence in one's native land
16. Disposed towards evil
19. Period during which something is held
20. Carefree & lighthearted
21. Having no useful result

Great Expectations Vocabulary Crossword 2 Answer Key

Across
1. Arrogant; insulting
4. Melancholy; gloomy
6. Fever & chills
7. Relating to marriage
10. One tenth
11. Totally reject
14. Damaging
17. Easily understood
18. Present but not active; hidden
21. Pleased; willing; obliged
22. Make a statement of facts
23. Having a tendency to fight; fierce
24. Letter

Down
1. At odds; not matching
2. Summary
3. Predict
5. Arousing strong dislike
6. Suggested indirectly
8. Without a conscience or a moral code
9. Hint
12. Release from an entanglement
13. Generous in forgiving; noble
15. Removed from residence in one's native land
16. Disposed towards evil
19. Period during which something is held
20. Carefree & lighthearted
21. Having no useful result

Great Expectations Vocabulary Crossword 3

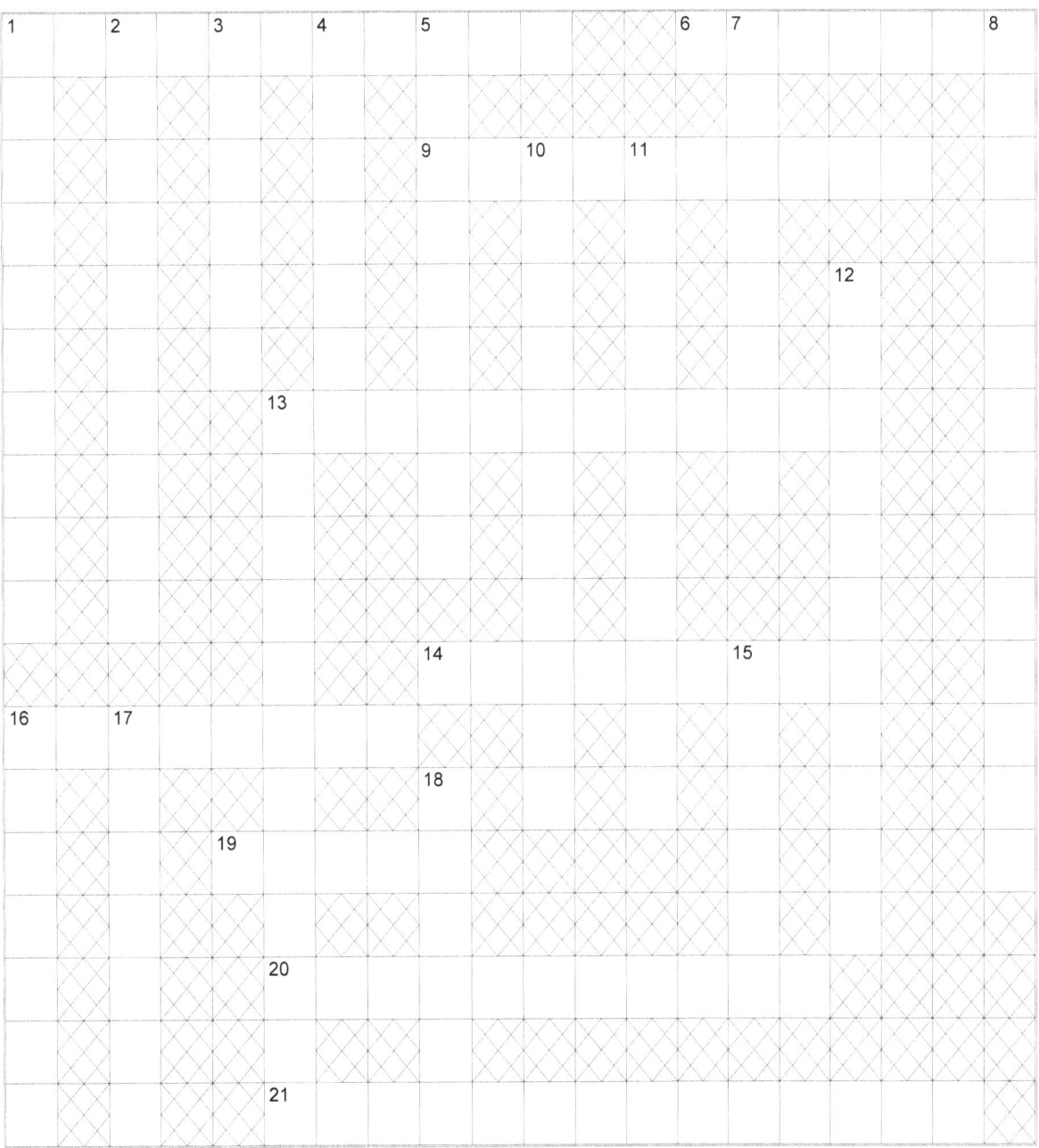

Across
1. Approval
6. Braided
9. Destructive; deadly
13. Sense that something is about to happen
14. Release from an entanglement
16. Condition of being temporarily set aside
19. One tenth
20. At odds; not matching
21. Showing haughty disdain

Down
1. Consented without argument
2. Most common; widespread
3. Arousing strong dislike
4. Apart from each other
5. Lacking reverence, respect or dutifulness
7. Dawdled; proceeded slowly or with many stops
8. Gloomily
10. Make a preliminary investigation
11. Complexities
12. Damaging
13. Tendencies
15. Contemptible; miserable; wretched
16. Suggested indirectly
17. Letter
18. Make a statement of facts

Great Expectations Vocabulary Crossword 3 Answer Key

Across
1. Approval
6. Braided
9. Destructive; deadly
13. Sense that something is about to happen
14. Release from an entanglement
16. Condition of being temporarily set aside
19. One tenth
20. At odds; not matching
21. Showing haughty disdain

Down
1. Consented without argument
2. Most common; widespread
3. Arousing strong dislike
4. Apart from each other
5. Lacking reverence, respect or dutifulness
7. Dawdled; proceeded slowly or with many stops
8. Gloomily
10. Make a preliminary investigation
11. Complexities
12. Damaging
13. Tendencies
15. Contemptible; miserable; wretched
16. Suggested indirectly
17. Letter
18. Make a statement of facts

Great Expectations Vocabulary Crossword 4

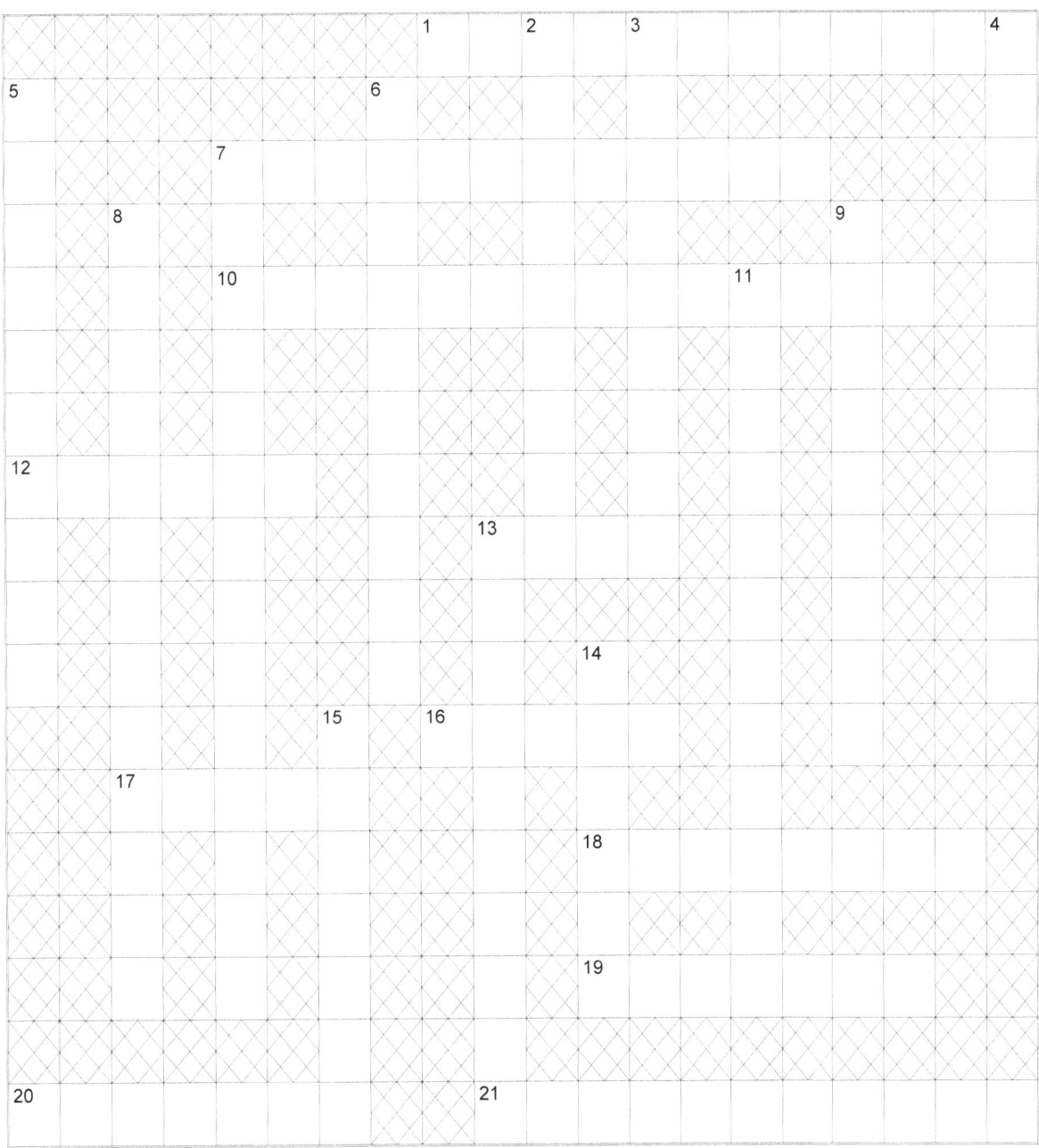

Across
1. Sense that something is about to happen
7. Belittling
10. Showing haughty disdain
12. Present but not active; hidden
13. Fever & chills
16. Predict
17. One tenth
18. Arrogant; insulting
19. Letter
20. Braided
21. Damaging

Down
2. Bringing out; drawing forth
3. Release from an entanglement
4. State of dread or alarm
5. Most common; widespread
6. Undecided
7. Gloomily
8. State of paralyzing dismay
9. Turn away; push away
11. Without a conscience or a moral code
13. Consented without argument
14. Having no useful result
15. Looked over with care

Great Expectations Vocabulary Crossword 4 Answer Key

Across
1. Sense that something is about to happen
7. Belittling
10. Showing haughty disdain
12. Present but not active; hidden
13. Fever & chills
16. Predict
17. One tenth
18. Arrogant; insulting
19. Letter
20. Braided
21. Damaging

Down
2. Bringing out; drawing forth
3. Release from an entanglement
4. State of dread or alarm
5. Most common; widespread
6. Undecided
7. Gloomily
8. State of paralyzing dismay
9. Turn away; push away
11. Without a conscience or a moral code
13. Consented without argument
14. Having no useful result
15. Looked over with care

Great Expectations Vocabulary Juggle Letters 1

1. CGLTINIIE   = 1. _____
                       Bringing out; drawing forth

2. NRUEISIPCO   = 2. _____
                       Destructive; deadly

3. TCERAXTIE   = 3. _____
                       Release from an entanglement

4. EOSUBUQOIS   = 4. _____
                       Full of or showing servile compliance

5. NIGDCOENS   = 5. _____
                       Entrusted; gave over to the care of another

6. DUCSEICQEA   = 6. _____
                       Consented without argument

7. SANIICCRIET   = 7. _____
                       Complexities

8. NMTTOOPNIE   = 8. _____
                       All-powerful

9. SIUYLMOIP   = 9. _____
                       Lacking reverence, respect or dutifulness

10. TPREXAEDIAT   =10. _____
                       Removed from residence in one's native land

11. REDPVEA   =11. _____
                       Be present throughout

12. ETTCNNNSOIRAO =12. _____
                       State of paralyzing dismay

13. OTEERHXD   =13. _____
                       Urged; advised

14. IIOSAURCCP   =14. _____
                       Whimsical

15. NIPIDETAEOCR =15. _____
                       Belittling

Great Expectations Vocabulary Juggle Letters 1 Answer Key

1. CGLTINIIE = 1. ELICITING
   Bringing out; drawing forth

2. NRUEISIPCO = 2. PERNICIOUS
   Destructive; deadly

3. TCERAXTIE = 3. EXTRICATE
   Release from an entanglement

4. EOSUBUQOIS = 4. OBSEQUIOUS
   Full of or showing servile compliance

5. NIGDCOENS = 5. CONSIGNED
   Entrusted; gave over to the care of another

6. DUCSEICQEA = 6. ACQUIESCED
   Consented without argument

7. SANIICCRIET = 7. INTRICACIES
   Complexities

8. NMTTOOPNIE = 8. OMNIPOTENT
   All-powerful

9. SIUYLMOIP = 9. IMPIOUSLY
   Lacking reverence, respect or dutifulness

10. TPREXAEDIAT = 10. EXPATRIATED
    Removed from residence in one's native land

11. REDPVEA = 11. PERVADE
    Be present throughout

12. ETTCNNNSOIRAO = 12. CONSTERNATION
    State of paralyzing dismay

13. OTEERHXD = 13. EXHORTED
    Urged; advised

14. IIOSAURCCP = 14. CAPRICIOUS
    Whimsical

15. NIPIDETAEOCR = 15. DEPRECIATION
    Belittling

Great Expectations Vocabulary Juggle Letters 2

1. RNNGICOYUIT   = 1. _____
                      At odds; not matching

2. IFNA   = 2. _____
                      Pleased; willing; obliged

3. SIUAIOVARC   = 3. _____
                      Stingy; wanting wealth for oneself

4. NLTOEEENVB   = 4. _____
                      Good

5. TSIDAIYSU   = 5. _____
                      Constant personal attention

6. YELLISSROPCUUI = 6. _____
                      Showing haughty disdain

7. MONTTIIIAN   = 7. _____
                      Hint

8. EOOMRS   = 8. _____
                      Melancholy; gloomy

9. UNSANMIGOMA   = 9. _____
                      Generous in forgiving; noble

10. ESLIREORUT   =10. _____
                      Undecided

11. TGNAANLIM   =11. _____
                      Disposed towards evil

12. ELELNIIDB   =12. _____
                      Permanent

13. CSYAAOLSUGI   =13. _____
                      Intelligently; wisely

14. IPTEREDAXTA   =14. _____
                      Removed from residence in one's native land

15. ELNIATDRMET   =15. _____
                      Damaging

Great Expectations Vocabulary Juggle Letters 2 Answer Key

1. RNNGICOYUIT = 1. INCONGRUITY
   At odds; not matching

2. IFNA = 2. FAIN
   Pleased; willing; obliged

3. SIUAIOVARC = 3. AVARICIOUS
   Stingy; wanting wealth for oneself

4. NLTOEEENVB = 4. BENEVOLENT
   Good

5. TSIDAIYSU = 5. ASSIDUITY
   Constant personal attention

6. YELLISSROPCUUI = 6. SUPERCILIOUSLY
   Showing haughty disdain

7. MONTTIIIAN = 7. INTIMATION
   Hint

8. EOOMRS = 8. MOROSE
   Melancholy; gloomy

9. UNSANMIGOMA = 9. MAGNANIMOUS
   Generous in forgiving; noble

10. ESLIREORUT = 10. IRRESOLUTE
    Undecided

11. TGNAANLIM = 11. MALIGNANT
    Disposed towards evil

12. ELELNIIDB = 12. INDELIBLE
    Permanent

13. CSYAAOLSUGI = 13. SAGACIOUSLY
    Intelligently; wisely

14. IPTEREDAXTA = 14. EXPATRIATED
    Removed from residence in one's native land

15. ELNIATDRMET = 15. DETRIMENTAL
    Damaging

Great Expectations Vocabulary Juggle Letters 3

1. XDOHEETR = 1. _____
   Urged; advised

2. SNLNOTYEIL = 2. _____
   Insultingly; rudely

3. UOLSYIIERPM = 3. _____
   Domineeringly; overbearingly

4. IAPPTARION = 4. _____
   Ghost

5. IEECNXRTAG = 5. _____
   Cursing

6. BATECJ = 6. _____
   Contemptible; miserable; wretched

7. NLIEBLDIE = 7. _____
   Permanent

8. OESOMR = 8. _____
   Melancholy; gloomy

9. ROTEIIEDNPAC = 9. _____
   Belittling

10. NURTEE =10. _____
    Period during which something is held

11. TYNEAOLOSCSLID =11. _____
    Gloomily

12. UOSNAYRVEL =12. _____
    Hungrily

13. OONSTICUGU =13. _____
    Neighboring; adjacent

14. SMOYIILPU =14. _____
    Lacking reverence, respect or dutifulness

15. URAGU =15. _____
    Predict

Great Expectations Vocabulary Juggle Letters 3 Answer Key

1. XDOHEETR = 1. EXHORTED
   Urged; advised

2. SNLNOTYEIL = 2. INSOLENTLY
   Insultingly; rudely

3. UOLSYIIERPM = 3. IMPERIOUSLY
   Domineeringly; overbearingly

4. IAPPTARION = 4. APPARITION
   Ghost

5. IEECNXRTAG = 5. EXCREATING
   Cursing

6. BATECJ = 6. ABJECT
   Contemptible; miserable; wretched

7. NLIEBLDIE = 7. INDELIBLE
   Permanent

8. OESOMR = 8. MOROSE
   Melancholy; gloomy

9. ROTEIIEDNPAC = 9. DEPRECIATION
   Belittling

10. NURTEE = 10. TENURE
    Period during which something is held

11. TYNEAOLOSCSLID = 11. DISCONSOLATELY
    Gloomily

12. UOSNAYRVEL = 12. RAVENOUSLY
    Hungrily

13. OONSTICUGU = 13. CONTIGUOUS
    Neighboring; adjacent

14. SMOYIILPU = 14. IMPIOUSLY
    Lacking reverence, respect or dutifulness

15. URAGU = 15. AUGUR
    Predict

Great Expectations Vocabulary Jugle Letters 4

1. DSUEEPR = 1. _____
Looked over with care

2. HBLTEI = 2. _____
Carefree & lighthearted

3. YIAOLTEBSNT = 3. _____
Stubbornly

4. ITTEH = 4. _____
One tenth

5. TCINEETR = 5. _____
Reserved

6. SNDOCTROE = 6. _____
Associated

7. LNSITNOE = 7. _____
Arrogant; insulting

8. VNENELETBO = 8. _____
Good

9. ISISYTADU = 9. _____
Constant personal attention

10. NTECORERONI =10. _____
Make a preliminary investigation

11. ATNCRNETH =11. _____
Distinct; forceful, effective & vigorous

12. AIFN =12. _____
Pleased; willing; obliged

13. IIRAOUSVAC =13. _____
Stingy; wanting wealth for oneself

14. ETLSRRUEIO =14. _____
Undecided

15. QEECIDSUCA =15. _____
Consented without argument

Great Expectations Vocabulary Juggle Letters 4 Answer Key

1. DSUEEPR = 1. PERUSED
Looked over with care

2. HBLTEI = 2. BLITHE
Carefree & lighthearted

3. YIAOLTEBSNT = 3. OBSTINATELY
Stubbornly

4. ITTEH = 4. TITHE
One tenth

5. TCINEETR = 5. RETICENT
Reserved

6. SNDOCTROE = 6. CONSORTED
Associated

7. LNSITNOE = 7. INSOLENT
Arrogant; insulting

8. VNENELETBO = 8. BENEVOLENT
Good

9. ISISYTADU = 9. ASSIDUITY
Constant personal attention

10. NTECORERONI = 10. RECONNOITRE
Make a preliminary investigation

11. ATNCRNETH = 11. TRENCHANT
Distinct; forceful, effective & vigorous

12. AIFN = 12. FAIN
Pleased; willing; obliged

13. IIRAOUSVAC = 13. AVARICIOUS
Stingy; wanting wealth for oneself

14. ETLSRRUEIO = 14. IRRESOLUTE
Undecided

15. QEECIDSUCA = 15. ACQUIESCED
Consented without argument

ABEYANCE	Condition of being temporarily set aside
ABJECT	Contemptible; miserable; wretched
ACQUIESCED	Consented without argument
AGUE	Fever & chills
ALIENATED	Turned away; pushed away
ALLUDED	Suggested indirectly

APPARITION	Ghost
APPROBATION	Approval
ASSIDUITY	Constant personal attention
ASUNDER	Apart from each other
AUGMENTED	Added to
AUGUR	Predict

AUSPICIOUS	Marked by success; grand
AVARICIOUS	Stingy; wanting wealth for oneself
BENEVOLENT	Good
BLITHE	Carefree & lighthearted
CAPRICIOUS	Whimsical
CONNUBIAL	Relating to marriage

CONSIGNED	Entrusted; gave over to the care of another
CONSORTED	Associated
CONSTERNATION	State of paralyzing dismay
CONTIGUOUS	Neighboring; adjacent
CORROBORATED	Supported by other evidence
COUNTENANCES	Faces

DEPOSE	Make a statement of facts
DEPRECIATION	Belittling
DETRIMENTAL	Damaging
DISCONSOLATELY	Gloomily
ELICITING	Bringing out; drawing forth
EPISTLE	Letter

EXCREATING	Cursing
EXECRATED	Denounced
EXHORTED	Urged; advised
EXONERATED	Freed from blame
EXPATRIATED	Removed from residence in one's native land
EXTRICATE	Release from an entanglement

FAIN	Pleased; willing; obliged
FELICITOUS	Lucky
FIDELITY	Faithfulness; loyalty
FORTUITOUSLY	By accident or chance
FUTILE	Having no useful result
IGNOMINIOUSLY	Shamefully; humiliatingly

IMPERIOUSLY	Domineeringly; overbearingly
IMPETUOSITY	Forcefully; passionately
IMPIOUSLY	Lacking reverence, respect or dutifulness
INCONGRUITY	At odds; not matching
INDELIBLE	Permanent
INSOLENT	Arrogant; insulting

INSOLENTLY	Insultingly; rudely
INTIMATION	Hint
INTRICACIES	Complexities
IRRESOLUTE	Undecided
LATENT	Present but not active; hidden
LOITERED	Dawdled; proceeded slowly or with many stops

LUCID	Easily understood
MAGNANIMOUS	Generous in forgiving; noble
MALIGNANT	Disposed towards evil
MOROSE	Melancholy; gloomy
OBDURATE	Hard-hearted; not giving in to persuasion
OBSEQUIOUS	Full of or showing servile compliance

OBSTINATELY	Stubbornly
ODIOUS	Arousing strong dislike
OMNIPOTENT	All-powerful
PERNICIOUS	Destructive; deadly
PERUSED	Looked over with care
PERVADE	Be present throughout

PLAITED	Braided
PRESENTIMENT	Sense that something is about to happen
PREVAILING	Most common; widespread
PROPENSITIES	Tendencies
RAVENOUSLY	Hungrily
RECONNOITRE	Make a preliminary investigation

REFECTORIES	Rooms where meals are served
REPUDIATE	Totally reject
RETICENT	Reserved
SAGACIOUSLY	Intelligently; wisely
SUPERCILIOUSLY	Showing haughty disdain
SYNOPSIS	Summary

TENURE	Period during which something is held
TITHE	One tenth
TRENCHANT	Distinct; forceful, effective & vigorous
TREPIDATION	State of dread or alarm
TRUCULENT	Having a tendency to fight; fierce
UNSCRUPULOUS	Without a conscience or a moral code

Great Expectations Vocabulary

IMPIOUSLY	MAGNANIMOUS	RECONNOITRE	EXPATRIATED	TRUCULENT
MOROSE	SYNOPSIS	EXONERATED	EXCREATING	MALIGNANT
EXTRICATE	IGNOMINIOUSLY	FREE SPACE	BLITHE	EXECRATED
OMNIPOTENT	ABJECT	ASSIDUITY	ELICITING	APPROBATION
EPISTLE	ABEYANCE	EXHORTED	APPARITION	FUTILE

Great Expectations Vocabulary

OBSTINATELY	ODIOUS	COUNTENANCES	CONSORTED	DEPOSE
AGUE	IMPERIOUSLY	INTRICACIES	CONSIGNED	LUCID
SUPERCILIOUSLY	ALIENATED	FREE SPACE	CONTIGUOUS	PLAITED
CORROBORATED	AUGMENTED	ALLUDED	CONNUBIAL	PROPENSITIES
FIDELITY	INTIMATION	UNSCRUPULOUS	INCONGRUITY	TENURE

Great Expectations Vocabulary

CORROBORATED	RAVENOUSLY	OBSEQUIOUS	DETRIMENTAL	EXECRATED
ODIOUS	FELICITOUS	APPROBATION	DEPOSE	EPISTLE
AUGMENTED	ASSIDUITY	FREE SPACE	ABEYANCE	IRRESOLUTE
ALIENATED	ABJECT	IMPERIOUSLY	FAIN	TRENCHANT
RETICENT	MALIGNANT	IMPETUOSITY	EXHORTED	EXTRICATE

Great Expectations Vocabulary

TITHE	DISCONSOLATELY	RECONNOITRE	REFECTORIES	OMNIPOTENT
LOITERED	PERVADE	OBSTINATELY	AVARICIOUS	MAGNANIMOUS
UNSCRUPULOUS	TRUCULENT	FREE SPACE	IGNOMINIOUSLY	AUGUR
CONTIGUOUS	PLAITED	AGUE	EXONERATED	BENEVOLENT
PERUSED	ELICITING	ASUNDER	INTRICACIES	TREPIDATION

Great Expectations Vocabulary

FIDELITY	DEPOSE	PROPENSITIES	CORROBORATED	CONSORTED
FORTUITOUSLY	INCONGRUITY	ALIENATED	ASUNDER	REPUDIATE
APPROBATION	OMNIPOTENT	FREE SPACE	EXPATRIATED	DISCONSOLATELY
EXHORTED	SYNOPSIS	COUNTENANCES	RECONNOITRE	EPISTLE
INSOLENTLY	PLAITED	INDELIBLE	LUCID	RAVENOUSLY

Great Expectations Vocabulary

RETICENT	ACQUIESCED	MALIGNANT	BENEVOLENT	TRENCHANT
TITHE	MOROSE	OBSTINATELY	CONSIGNED	AUGUR
CONSTERNATION	INTRICACIES	FREE SPACE	FELICITOUS	ALLUDED
IMPETUOSITY	IRRESOLUTE	TENURE	APPARITION	LOITERED
OBDURATE	DEPRECIATION	EXCREATING	FAIN	AGUE

Great Expectations Vocabulary

CONTIGUOUS	TRENCHANT	IMPERIOUSLY	AUGUR	MOROSE
INSOLENT	REPUDIATE	EXHORTED	INTIMATION	IMPETUOSITY
PERUSED	EXONERATED	FREE SPACE	UNSCRUPULOUS	DEPOSE
PERNICIOUS	ABEYANCE	CONSORTED	RAVENOUSLY	SYNOPSIS
PRESENTIMENT	CAPRICIOUS	ALLUDED	MAGNANIMOUS	ABJECT

Great Expectations Vocabulary

AGUE	FIDELITY	PLAITED	INTRICACIES	APPARITION
CORROBORATED	DEPRECIATION	EXTRICATE	PROPENSITIES	OBSEQUIOUS
AVARICIOUS	PREVAILING	FREE SPACE	LATENT	CONSTERNATION
ALIENATED	ASSIDUITY	APPROBATION	EXECRATED	SUPERCILIOUSLY
PERVADE	EPISTLE	DISCONSOLATELY	MALIGNANT	TRUCULENT

Great Expectations Vocabulary

ACQUIESCED	DETRIMENTAL	FORTUITOUSLY	EXCREATING	LOITERED
MALIGNANT	RECONNOITRE	APPARITION	INDELIBLE	DISCONSOLATELY
RETICENT	ASSIDUITY	FREE SPACE	IMPERIOUSLY	REPUDIATE
INCONGRUITY	ABEYANCE	FUTILE	AUSPICIOUS	CONSORTED
DEPRECIATION	SUPERCILIOUSLY	TENURE	IMPIOUSLY	BENEVOLENT

Great Expectations Vocabulary

LUCID	EPISTLE	CONTIGUOUS	IGNOMINIOUSLY	PLAITED
ODIOUS	APPROBATION	TITHE	ASUNDER	AUGUR
ALLUDED	RAVENOUSLY	FREE SPACE	OBDURATE	PERUSED
EXPATRIATED	IRRESOLUTE	FELICITOUS	CAPRICIOUS	CORROBORATED
DEPOSE	ALIENATED	AUGMENTED	LATENT	SYNOPSIS

Great Expectations Vocabulary

SUPERCILIOUSLY	MAGNANIMOUS	DEPOSE	RETICENT	DEPRECIATION
RAVENOUSLY	TENURE	AUGUR	BLITHE	COUNTENANCES
FAIN	EXHORTED	FREE SPACE	ELICITING	ACQUIESCED
INDELIBLE	ASSIDUITY	CONSORTED	EPISTLE	CONTIGUOUS
INCONGRUITY	INSOLENT	PROPENSITIES	LATENT	TITHE

Great Expectations Vocabulary

MALIGNANT	CAPRICIOUS	OBSEQUIOUS	EXECRATED	PERNICIOUS
OBSTINATELY	FORTUITOUSLY	MOROSE	AUGMENTED	RECONNOITRE
LOITERED	APPROBATION	FREE SPACE	INTIMATION	EXONERATED
AVARICIOUS	ABEYANCE	CORROBORATED	IMPERIOUSLY	IMPETUOSITY
EXCREATING	INTRICACIES	TRUCULENT	ASUNDER	SAGACIOUSLY

Great Expectations Vocabulary

REPUDIATE	IRRESOLUTE	FORTUITOUSLY	REFECTORIES	INDELIBLE
UNSCRUPULOUS	FIDELITY	RECONNOITRE	ELICITING	TRENCHANT
BLITHE	PERNICIOUS	FREE SPACE	INTIMATION	CONNUBIAL
LATENT	IMPIOUSLY	ALIENATED	AUSPICIOUS	AUGUR
DISCONSOLATELY	PRESENTIMENT	DEPRECIATION	COUNTENANCES	AUGMENTED

Great Expectations Vocabulary

ASSIDUITY	SUPERCILIOUSLY	PREVAILING	EXHORTED	RETICENT
EXTRICATE	APPARITION	RAVENOUSLY	INSOLENTLY	AVARICIOUS
CORROBORATED	IMPERIOUSLY	FREE SPACE	INCONGRUITY	FAIN
OBSEQUIOUS	FELICITOUS	OBDURATE	EXCREATING	APPROBATION
EXPATRIATED	PROPENSITIES	ODIOUS	PERVADE	ABEYANCE

Great Expectations Vocabulary

REPUDIATE	IMPETUOSITY	PRESENTIMENT	CONSORTED	EXTRICATE
FAIN	ACQUIESCED	SUPERCILIOUSLY	SYNOPSIS	EPISTLE
CONSIGNED	IRRESOLUTE	FREE SPACE	FUTILE	TREPIDATION
ELICITING	INTIMATION	INSOLENT	MAGNANIMOUS	FIDELITY
CONTIGUOUS	INCONGRUITY	CONSTERNATION	UNSCRUPULOUS	ALIENATED

Great Expectations Vocabulary

RAVENOUSLY	OBSEQUIOUS	TRUCULENT	ASSIDUITY	MOROSE
ABJECT	IMPIOUSLY	AUSPICIOUS	COUNTENANCES	INDELIBLE
MALIGNANT	TENURE	FREE SPACE	BLITHE	IGNOMINIOUSLY
EXCREATING	REFECTORIES	DISCONSOLATELY	ABEYANCE	FELICITOUS
RETICENT	TITHE	CORROBORATED	FORTUITOUSLY	ODIOUS

Great Expectations Vocabulary

FORTUITOUSLY	ASSIDUITY	EXCREATING	RAVENOUSLY	EPISTLE
PROPENSITIES	EXONERATED	BENEVOLENT	INTIMATION	ALLUDED
EXPATRIATED	EXTRICATE	FREE SPACE	UNSCRUPULOUS	FELICITOUS
PERVADE	SAGACIOUSLY	ABEYANCE	TRENCHANT	COUNTENANCES
IRRESOLUTE	MAGNANIMOUS	RECONNOITRE	INSOLENT	OMNIPOTENT

Great Expectations Vocabulary

ELICITING	LATENT	FAIN	INTRICACIES	CONSORTED
CONSTERNATION	AVARICIOUS	INSOLENTLY	OBSTINATELY	MALIGNANT
IMPETUOSITY	REFECTORIES	FREE SPACE	AUSPICIOUS	PERNICIOUS
SYNOPSIS	OBDURATE	IMPIOUSLY	AUGMENTED	PLAITED
MOROSE	PERUSED	EXHORTED	LOITERED	FIDELITY

Great Expectations Vocabulary

RETICENT	REFECTORIES	EXTRICATE	CONTIGUOUS	OBSEQUIOUS
PREVAILING	IMPERIOUSLY	CONNUBIAL	CONSIGNED	ASSIDUITY
IMPETUOSITY	TRENCHANT	FREE SPACE	BENEVOLENT	AUGUR
APPARITION	PERUSED	LUCID	COUNTENANCES	ABJECT
ACQUIESCED	INDELIBLE	RAVENOUSLY	EXCREATING	FIDELITY

Great Expectations Vocabulary

IGNOMINIOULY	SAGACIOUSLY	PERVADE	EXONERATED	DEPOSE
FUTILE	IRRESOLUTE	AUGMENTED	INTRICACIES	REPUDIATE
ABEYANCE	ALLUDED	FREE SPACE	DISCONSOLATELY	MAGNANIMOUS
ELICITING	APPROBATION	ODIOUS	PERNICIOUS	INSOLENTLY
OBDURATE	OBSTINATELY	TENURE	BLITHE	EPISTLE

Great Expectations Vocabulary

DEPRECIATION	AUSPICIOUS	UNSCRUPULOUS	MOROSE	CONSTERNATION
ALLUDED	PRESENTIMENT	BLITHE	EXHORTED	CONNUBIAL
OBSEQUIOUS	COUNTENANCES	FREE SPACE	TENURE	INSOLENT
EXCREATING	AVARICIOUS	REPUDIATE	OBSTINATELY	INTRICACIES
INCONGRUITY	APPROBATION	DISCONSOLATELY	PERNICIOUS	EPISTLE

Great Expectations Vocabulary

APPARITION	SYNOPSIS	PERVADE	AGUE	IMPETUOSITY
FELICITOUS	FAIN	INTIMATION	CONSORTED	TRUCULENT
ACQUIESCED	BENEVOLENT	FREE SPACE	CONSIGNED	RAVENOUSLY
MAGNANIMOUS	EXONERATED	MALIGNANT	SUPERCILIOUSLY	EXTRICATE
LUCID	ODIOUS	FUTILE	DEPOSE	FIDELITY

Great Expectations Vocabulary

FAIN	CONSORTED	LOITERED	SYNOPSIS	CONSTERNATION
FELICITOUS	CONTIGUOUS	RETICENT	FUTILE	ABJECT
OBSTINATELY	MAGNANIMOUS	FREE SPACE	FORTUITOUSLY	EXONERATED
DEPOSE	FIDELITY	ALLUDED	ELICITING	LATENT
CONSIGNED	EPISTLE	IMPERIOUSLY	LUCID	IMPETUOSITY

Great Expectations Vocabulary

COUNTENANCES	PLAITED	APPROBATION	MOROSE	RAVENOUSLY
INDELIBLE	INCONGRUITY	IMPIOUSLY	ALIENATED	INSOLENT
SAGACIOUSLY	TENURE	FREE SPACE	INSOLENTLY	PRESENTIMENT
IRRESOLUTE	OBSEQUIOUS	CORROBORATED	AVARICIOUS	TREPIDATION
MALIGNANT	EXTRICATE	AUGUR	REPUDIATE	CAPRICIOUS

Great Expectations Vocabulary

CONSTERNATION	IGNOMINIOULY	DISCONSOLATELY	EXONERATED	AUGMENTED
PREVAILING	EPISTLE	SAGACIOUSLY	FIDELITY	IMPIOUSLY
AGUE	AUGUR	FREE SPACE	EXECRATED	DEPRECIATION
CONSIGNED	LOITERED	CORROBORATED	PERNICIOUS	TRENCHANT
BLITHE	ABEYANCE	TREPIDATION	EXCREATING	INSOLENT

Great Expectations Vocabulary

SYNOPSIS	INTIMATION	APPROBATION	INTRICACIES	REFECTORIES
LUCID	ALIENATED	EXTRICATE	COUNTENANCES	OBSTINATELY
APPARITION	ODIOUS	FREE SPACE	INDELIBLE	RECONNOITRE
IMPETUOSITY	FORTUITOUSLY	DETRIMENTAL	ASSIDUITY	ELICITING
ASUNDER	INCONGRUITY	REPUDIATE	TRUCULENT	MAGNANIMOUS

Great Expectations Vocabulary

PLAITED	EXPATRIATED	ODIOUS	EPISTLE	AUGUR
SAGACIOUSLY	RAVENOUSLY	IMPIOUSLY	PERNICIOUS	CORROBORATED
DISCONSOLATELY	CONSORTED	FREE SPACE	OBSTINATELY	DEPRECIATION
MOROSE	PERVADE	ABJECT	EXECRATED	EXCREATING
LOITERED	AUSPICIOUS	EXTRICATE	TENURE	BENEVOLENT

Great Expectations Vocabulary

TRUCULENT	ABEYANCE	CONSTERNATION	INSOLENTLY	BLITHE
APPROBATION	PROPENSITIES	COUNTENANCES	AUGMENTED	ASSIDUITY
IGNOMINIOUSLY	MALIGNANT	FREE SPACE	IMPETUOSITY	AGUE
FORTUITOUSLY	SUPERCILIOUSLY	REFECTORIES	PREVAILING	PERUSED
DETRIMENTAL	LUCID	DEPOSE	OBSEQUIOUS	ASUNDER

Great Expectations Vocabulary

TRENCHANT	ABEYANCE	ELICITING	PROPENSITIES	INDELIBLE
CONSTERNATION	DETRIMENTAL	ODIOUS	INTIMATION	EXONERATED
TREPIDATION	CONTIGUOUS	FREE SPACE	EXECRATED	LATENT
APPROBATION	TENURE	INSOLENT	MALIGNANT	BLITHE
EXCREATING	IMPERIOUSLY	IMPIOUSLY	APPARITION	COUNTENANCES

Great Expectations Vocabulary

IGNOMINIOUSLY	FAIN	IRRESOLUTE	RECONNOITRE	BENEVOLENT
ACQUIESCED	AVARICIOUS	OMNIPOTENT	EXTRICATE	EPISTLE
CAPRICIOUS	FORTUITOUSLY	FREE SPACE	EXHORTED	ABJECT
INTRICACIES	ASSIDUITY	PRESENTIMENT	TITHE	AGUE
RAVENOUSLY	CONSIGNED	AUSPICIOUS	FUTILE	SUPERCILIOUSLY

Great Expectations Vocabulary

EXPATRIATED	BENEVOLENT	APPROBATION	SYNOPSIS	EXECRATED
AGUE	ASUNDER	LATENT	INDELIBLE	LOITERED
LUCID	ALLUDED	FREE SPACE	OBDURATE	BLITHE
AUGMENTED	CONSORTED	TENURE	IRRESOLUTE	ALIENATED
ELICITING	TITHE	SAGACIOUSLY	CAPRICIOUS	MOROSE

Great Expectations Vocabulary

PERUSED	IMPERIOUSLY	INSOLENTLY	FIDELITY	COUNTENANCES
REFECTORIES	EXTRICATE	OMNIPOTENT	ACQUIESCED	ASSIDUITY
INCONGRUITY	INTRICACIES	FREE SPACE	UNSCRUPULOUS	TRENCHANT
EPISTLE	ABEYANCE	DISCONSOLATELY	AVARICIOUS	CORROBORATED
PRESENTIMENT	RETICENT	OBSTINATELY	PROPENSITIES	RECONNOITRE

www.ingramcontent.com/pod-product-compliance
Lightning Source LLC
Chambersburg PA
CBHW081452070526
44586CB00019B/2324